BRITISH AUTHORS
Introductory Critical Studies

WALTER SCOTT

WALTER SCOTT

ROBIN MAYHEAD

Reader in English Studies
University of Stirling

AT THE UNIVERSITY PRESS

Published by the Syndics of the Cambridge University Press
Bentley House, 200 Euston Road, London NW1 2DB
American Branch: 32 East 57th Street, New York, N.Y. 10022

Library of Congress Catalogue Card Number: 72–88622

ISBNS:
0 521 20115 2 hard covers
0 521 09781 9 paperback

Printed in Great Britain
by W & J Mackay Limited, Chatham

FOR MY MOTHER

General Preface

This study of Walter Scott is the sixth in a series of short introductory critical studies of the more important British authors. The aim of the series is to go straight to the authors' works; to discuss them directly with a maximum of attention to concrete detail; to say what they are and what they do, and to indicate a valuation. The general critical attitude implied in the series is set out at some length in my *Understanding Literature*. Great literature is taken to be to a large extent self-explanatory to the reader who will attend carefully enough to what it says. 'Background' study, whether biographical or historical, is not the concern of the series.

It is hoped that this approach will suit a number of kinds of reader, in particular the general reader who would like an introduction which talks about the works themselves; and the student who would like a general critical study as a starting point, intending to go on to read more specialized works later. Since 'background' is not erected as an insuperable obstacle, readers in other English-speaking countries, countries where English is a second language, or even those for whom English is a foreign language, should find the books helpful. In Britain and the Commonwealth, students and teachers in universities and in the higher forms of secondary schools will find that the authors chosen for treatment are those most often prescribed for study in public and university examinations.

The series could be described as an attempt to make available to a wide public the results of the literary criticism of the last thirty years, and especially the methods associated with Cambridge. If the result is an increase in the reading, with enjoyment and understanding, of the great works of English literature, the books will have fulfilled their wider purpose.

ROBIN MAYHEAD

Acknowledgements

I am indebted to the Editor of *The Library Review* for permission to reprint my notice of Ioan Williams's book in Chapter 7. Chapter 3 is a greatly expanded version of an article which first appeared in *Essays in Criticism*, while Chapter 4 includes a few passages based on parts of an essay, 'Scott and the Idea of Justice', which was written for an anthology entitled *Scott's Mind and Art*. I have to thank Mr F. W. Bateson for permission thus to use my material in respect of the former, and Professor A. N. Jeffares and Messrs Oliver and Boyd likewise in respect of the latter. My discussion of *The Antiquary* in Chapter 4 incorporates material used in a paper given at Edinburgh University during the Scott Bicentenary Conference in 1971, and I am grateful to the organizers for the opportunity given me to test my approach to the book on a public platform.

Contents

Note. All passages quoted from the Waverley Novels are taken from the Holyrood Edition (Gresham Publishing Co., London, n.d.), except in the case of *Old Mortality* where the text used is that of the Centenary Edition (Edinburgh, 1886), and page numbers refer to these texts. The chapter on the poetry makes use of *The Poetical Works of Sir Walter Scott*, with introduction by W. M. Rossetti (London, Ward Lock and Co., n.d.). Part of Chapter 7 originally appeared as a review of Ioan Williams (ed.), *Sir Walter Scott on Novelists and Fiction* (London, 1968), and all I have said about Scott as a critic refers to the material assembled in that volume.

1

Introductory

Until recently there would have been something rather odd about the appearance of a book on Scott in a series of this kind. 'The literary criticism of the last thirty years' has had little time for him, and very scant enthusiasm. Does this book mean, then, a change of front, a concession, or a rediscovery?

It means none of those things, except to the extent that the re-reading of however familiar an author must always involve some element of rediscovery. No doubt this has been the case in the preparation of this book. It does not mean, though, an exultant proclamation that a prolonged foray into Scott after unjust neglect has revealed achievement of a wholly unsuspected nature. I have been a reader of the Waverley Novels for some twenty years, enjoying and re-reading some of them very much more than others, and I do not offer this study as embodying that dramatically radical type of rediscovery for which 'conversion' is the popular word. Still less is the book meant as an obligatory concession to the fact that nowadays more and more critics are disposed to take Scott seriously. No wind of critical change is imposing a strategically opportune change of critical tack.

Nevertheless, the amount and kind of attention now being given to Scott do have a bearing on this study. In recent years at least three substantial books have been published, there have been several smaller works plus a quantity of articles, and 1971 saw a serious academic conference at the University of Edinburgh celebrating the bicentenary of his birth. All signs point to a Scott Revival, soon to be in full flood.

This book does not represent an abandonment to the current; nor, on the other hand, does it set out to debunk reawakening enthusiasm for Scott in itself. I start from the conviction that there are important and valuable things in his work, but in trying to put my case for this I shall keep in mind another belief: that if a Scott Revival is upon us, we must look very discriminatingly at just what is being revived.

At this point, however, discrimination must for a while be turned on the assumptions lurking behind my opening paragraphs. They may be roughly reduced to something like the following: Scott's status has been regarded as dubious for much of the twentieth century so far, and despite the promise of revival is controversial even today. No doubt some readers of middle age, bored long ago at school by *Kenilworth* or *The Talisman*, for instance, would think 'dubious' too charitable a word, for if literature has come to mean anything to them it is in spite of Scott rather than because of him. Yet there are others of around their generation whose similarly unhappy schoolroom experience made them assume that Scott was unworthy of their time when Jane Austen, George Eliot, Henry James, Joseph Conrad, and D. H. Lawrence were to be explored, who have found, sometimes by pure chance, sometimes by following up a stray critical remark which has struck them, either that the books they once found so tiresome were only partly representative, or that at school they had been offered representative and sophisticated works in an uncomprehending way.

Such readers almost always maintain strong reservations about large areas of Scott's output, ranging from a regard for perhaps one third of it, through the opinion that only a very few of the novels and next to none of the poems are worthwhile, to something approaching the view expressed in a footnote by F. R. Leavis:

Scott was primarily a kind of inspired folk-lorist, qualified to have done in fiction something analogous to the ballad-opera: the only live part of *Redgauntlet* now is 'Wandering Willie's Tale', and 'The Two Drovers' remains in esteem while the heroics of the historical novels no longer command respect. He was a great and very intelligent man; but, not having the creative writer's interest in literature, he made no serious attempt to work out his own form and break away from the bad tradition of the eighteenth-century romance. Of his books *The Heart of Midlothian* comes the nearest to being a great novel, but hardly *is* that: too many allowances and deductions have to be made. (*The Great Tradition* (London, 1948), p. 5.)

While not being absolutely dismissed, Scott is there firmly placed as having very limited significance in terms of positive achievement.

Somewhere between that view and the other positions I have roughly charted comes this, from a companion volume to the present book:

And while that part of Scott's enormous output that deals with the heroism and humanity of common people in a familiar setting shares today something of the critical acclaim accorded to Jane Austen's work, the reputation of his historical novels (so great in his and Jane Austen's time) has been seen to dwindle into comparative insignificance. (Yasmine Gooneratne, *Jane Austen* (Cambridge, 1970), p. 1.)

This study will certainly find itself considering the kind of truth that both passages contain, though this will only be after particular works have actually been considered. Meanwhile a question must be asked: Will the common assumption of the two critics that Scott's once immense reputation is today, for fairly obvious reasons, drastically diminished, be generally accepted or even understood?

Some suggestions have been made regarding the attitudes of older readers, but what of those who are a deal younger? *Kenilworth* and *The Talisman* no longer brood over schoolrooms far and wide. No more is Scott thought of as the ideally 'safe' and improving author for young minds. To many of the young, indeed, he is merely a name, and although some may have a vague notion that he is a bit of a bore they will not feel a dislike based on personal recollection. They will not necessarily be grateful to the teacher or critic who tells them that there is no harm in ignoring Scott, whereas their elders often gasped with incredulous relief at such tidings. Moreover, quite apart from the fact that Scott has not been impressed upon them as a 'figure', they may by no means think it axiomatic that the 'historical novel' is an inferior genre.

Now there is much to be thankful for in such reflections. A writer has everything to gain when his readers are uncorrupted by literary prejudices, and I hope that this book may urge some of the innocent in the direction of Scott. But literary prejudice can take many forms. There will only be loss, both for the reader's enjoyment and for Scott's reputation, if the Revival turns out to be the exhumation of dusty old bones, however many doctoral theses may be derived from them. An open-minded reader, downright bored by a bad Scott novel to which he has been sent by a zealous revivalist, will conclude that he has been sold a fake assiduously promulgated by the academic industry. He will not be surprised to hear older people recall with outrage the days when Scott was foisted upon them as a 'great' writer. Where, after all, lies the the difference between the old-style injunction to admire Scott's 'characters', for example, and a modishly new-style invitation to study his 'image-patterns', if the book in question is simply intolerable?

I think that the danger of Scott's reinstallation as a stock Great Name, honoured nowadays by up-to-date critical jargon but as big a bore as ever, quite alarmingly exists. Thus, although this book welcomes the unprejudiced reader and does not trouble to defend Scott against the more common charges of the pre-revival twentieth century, it does have a certain defensive function in view: to protect him against the claims of those who seek to give him the wrong kind of eminence, when the best service one can render him is to discriminate sharply. No one can afford to waste time on dry bones; there is more than enough real literature to be read.

Here a word of advance apology is needed – apology for referring again to other critics when the work of this book remains to be done. I hope this will be excused for the sake of the opportunity it affords conveniently to make a point fundamental to my undertaking. An anthology of essays which appeared in 1968 (D. D. Devlin (ed.), *Modern Judgements: Walter Scott* (London)), while containing some excellent material, has disquieting features. At the end of his introductory essay the editor approvingly quotes from a fellow enthusiast who argues *against* the contention that Scott is ill-served by those who take seriously works which have the reputation of being inferior, and proposes that one should approach such books 'on what appear to be their own terms'. 'And this,' he says, 'means avoiding many familiar traps, refusing to condemn the self-effacing Scott out of his own mouth, and trying not to defend him on grounds partly or wholly irrelevant.' To this the editor adds, 'It means, in fact, giving Scott something of the critical attention and intelligence that has been lavished on other novelists in the past thirty years.'

Such sentiments are admirable in themselves: admirable in laying stress on sensible standards of judgement, and in warning us not to be misled by Scott's own remarks about his careless habits in composition. But there lurks within those words '*on what appear to be their own terms*' an implicit danger, a danger exemplified here and there by some of the articles in the volume itself. An essay on *Ivanhoe*, for instance, points to parallels between what many have seen merely as a 'boy's book' and other Scott novels which may be accepted with a more ready seriousness, yet fails, for me, to make a case for regarding that work as really interesting in itself, parallels or no parallels. The demonstration that *Ivanhoe* is 'about' some of the same things as, say, *Rob Roy*, does not rescue the prose of its tournaments and catastrophes from being a turgid bore. And while it would be monstrous to deny the importance of disengaging what a novel is most centrally 'about' as a means of finding one's way into the work as a whole, it must be regarded strictly as a preliminary tactic, in no way to be taken as an easy substitute for total response. If what appear to be *Ivanhoe's* 'own terms' are of any importance, they must be terms in which the author's intelligence and sensitivity show themselves, as sometimes, even in that novel, they do. But clearly the phrase 'on what appear to be their own terms', pushed to an extreme, could justify sheer rubbish.

Ivanhoe is not sheer rubbish, but this study assumes that such interest as it has, together with that of similar historical fantasias, is more rewardingly apparent elsewhere. Though the curious reader may in time want to look at such works, I believe that the job of discrimination, in the hope that this will do Scott positive good, may best be performed in terms of far more immediately interesting novels. At the same time I wish it to be stressed that *Ivanhoe* and the like are not being ignored because they are 'historical', for that would be to fall into the facile assumption regarding the historical novel already queried. Scott at his best is 'historical' in the way that Dickens, George Eliot, and Thomas Hardy are, in that he brings alive the movements and tensions that

5

have shaped a society and continue to shape it. He is very much concerned with tradition, and with the forces which make against it. But what I have called historical fantasias (and I am thinking of books like *Kenilworth*, *The Talisman*, *The Betrothed*, and *Count Robert of Paris*, as well as *Ivanhoe*), though aspects of them almost inevitably overlap with interests in the major novels, are altogether more remote from the living realities of Scott's own time, let alone our own, and point forward to the historical best-seller of the twentieth century, whose 'history' is simply a matter of evoking the past for its own exotic Technicolor sake.

But now something must be said about the plan of this book, and its terms of reference. Despite my fears about the wrong kind of Scott Revival, I certainly cannot claim that my intention of being discriminating is in itself original. The most rewarding of Scott's recent critics are precisely those who believe that the only way to interest people in him is to get rid of the dead or doubtful wood. Broadly speaking their principle of discrimination has been the view that his best works are those which deal wholly or mainly with Scotland and with periods not too distant from his own life-time. I have myself followed that principle in the past, and I do not reject it now. But, like all literary assumptions, it runs the risk of degenerating into unquestioned cliché.

Therefore, although the view of Scott's successes as being mainly 'Scottish-based', so to speak, will no doubt emerge from this book as still a sound one, I have been at some pains to avoid making it central. One result is that despite the highly selective list of novels treated, some have been included which are not among those invariably favoured by the revivalists of today. The disposition of books over chapters, moreover, has not necessarily been dictated by the more obvious kinds of preoccupation they possess. While it is true that *Waverley*, *Rob Roy*, and *Redgauntlet*, share rebellion, real or planned, as one common theme, they will not be taken as a group, as I want to stress what seems to me each book's individual quality and distinct centre of interest. This may lead at times to emphases a little at odds with some current approaches, but they are not proposed irresponsibly. The principal aim of the study is to rouse interest in the newcomer by way of scrutiny of particular works, and it will be so much the better if it can provoke fresh responses in readers who already have some acquaintance with Scott.

The next two chapters will consider in some detail a pair of novels chosen as most idiosyncratically illustrating varied aspects of Scott's preoccupations and techniques. Thereafter groups of other novels will be more briefly discussed in the light of what seem to be his own best standards, and the final chapters will attempt to assess the place he has for the modern reader as poet and critic.

Before ending the present chapter, however, and as a means of leading into the body of the book, let us take a look at a specific passage of Scott's prose to offset the foregoing pages of generalization. Here is the portrait of King James I from a sometimes brilliant novel, *The Fortunes of Nigel*:

He was deeply learned, without possessing useful knowledge; sagacious in many individual cases, without having real wisdom; fond of his power, and desirous to maintain and augment it, yet willing to resign the direction of that, and of himself, to the most unworthy favourites; a big and bold asserter of his rights in words, yet one who tamely saw them trampled on in deeds; a lover of negotiations, in which he was always outwitted; and one who feared war, where conquest might have been easy. He was fond of his dignity, while he was perpetually degrading it by undue familiarity; capable of much public labour, yet often neglecting it for the meanest amusement; a wit, though a pedant; and a scholar, though fond of the conversation of the ignorant and uneducated. Even his timidity of temper was not uniform; and there were moments of his life, and those critical, in which he showed the spirit of his ancestors. He was laborious in trifles, and a trifler where serious labour was required; devout in his sentiments, and yet too often profane in his language; just and beneficent by nature, he yet gave way to the iniquities and oppression of others. He was penurious respecting money which he had to give from his own hand, yet inconsiderately and unboundedly profuse of that which he did not see. In a word, those good qualities which displayed themselves in particular cases and occasions, were not of a nature sufficiently firm and comprehensive to regulate his general conduct; and, showing themselves as they occasionally did, only entitled James to the character bestowed on him by Sully – that he was the wisest fool in Christendom.

That is writing of splendid authority; pointed yet expansive, weighty yet urbane. But to describe it like that is by no means to hold it up for admiration merely as a specimen of 'style', for the felicities of the language are inseparably bound up with the activity of a lively, judging intelligence. The impression of *rightness* in the wording, of a neat symmetry in the constructions, reflects a fair, flexible, yet firm mind in the author, intent upon a portrait that may give some notion of his sitter's manifold complexities.

Thus the many antitheses are not a mere stylistic trick designed to produce a surface effect of elegance, but are a natural outgrowth of the critically assessing intelligence. To take just one of them: 'He was laborious in trifles, and a trifler where serious labour was required.' That is not simply pretty, but facile, verbal juggling; the second half of the antithesis is not just a clever though pointless echoing of the first. 'He was *laborious* in trifles', with its heavy spoken stress on the adjective (the passage should be read aloud to be fully enjoyed), gives a sense of ponderously doddering absurdity. The tone is amused, if a little contemptuous. But in the second half it becomes really scornful: 'and a *trifler* where *serious labour* was required'. If we normally think of 'trifles' merely as things that we do not take seriously, a '*trifler*', on the other hand, is more than likely to be a person of whom we definitely disapprove. And that is certainly the way in which Scott reacts to James at this point. The king emerges here as not only absurd but morally reprehensible into the bargain. Faced with the demanded and the demanding, he can do nothing but play about, and this qualifies what had been mainly amusement at his heavy bumbling over matters of no importance. By his deft opposition of 'trifles' and 'trifler', 'laborious' and 'labour', Scott attains an ironic vigour reflecting a play of mind that is both serious and amused, caught in the tight structure of pointed aphorism.

One could comment on many effective things in the passage. There is the characterization of James as 'a *big* and *bold* asserter of his rights in words', where the alliteration suggests blustering inflation until it collapses into the deflating effect of 'tamely saw them trampled on in deeds'. Even the repeated use of the word 'fond', which could at first suggest a lack of variety in the prose, becomes a virtue when we remember the old link between 'fond' and 'foolish'. The whole passage, indeed, moves superbly to-

INTRODUCTORY

wards that final summing-up of the king as 'the wisest fool in Christendom'. Above all the writing impresses by its balanced fairness, with the sense one feels of Scott's positive relish in depicting so contradictory a man. And it is from that appetite for the complex and contradictory that the next chapter begins.

9

2

'Waverley'

In the history of Scotland which he published under the title *Tales of a Grandfather*, Scott has this to say about the Union that joined the formerly separate kingdoms of England and Scotland under one government:

On the 1st of May 1707 the Union took place, amid the dejection and despair which attend on the downfall of an ancient state, and under a sullen expression of discontent that was far from promising the course of prosperity which the treaty finally produced.

And here I must point out to you at some length that, although there could never be a doubt that the Union in itself was a most desirable event, yet by the erroneous mode in which it was pushed on and opposed by all parties concerned, such obstacles were thrown in the way of the benefits it was calculated to produce as to interpose a longer interval of years betwixt the date of the treaty and the national advantages arising out of it, than the term spent by the Jews in the wilderness ere they attained the promised land.

The second paragraph is especially interesting, for although it has the air of simply being emphatic explanation, designed to avoid misunderstanding of the Union's real implications, its tone suggests very mixed feelings in the author himself. After all the melancholy surrounding 'the downfall of an ancient state', Scott seems rather suspiciously anxious to rush totally committed to the Union's defence, with that urgent '*And here I must point out to you at some length*'. He is particular to put the blame for trouble upon the 'parties concerned' rather than on the idea of Union itself, yet it is hard not to feel that he may be doing this to reassure himself, as well as the reader, that the event was indeed 'most desirable'.

That hint of ambiguity is highly characteristic not only of the attitudes of Scott himself, but the attitudes of others towards him. In the heyday of his nineteenth-century fame he was thought of very much as a classic of 'English' literature, a view which extended well into the present century, as many older readers would testify. And while that way of looking at him is no longer orthodox, there are today not a few people intensely interested in the literature of Scotland who would question his claim to be regarded, properly speaking, as a Scottish author specifically. Yet, though Scott would probably not have minded overmuch about which shelf he was placed upon as an *author*, his letters and *Journal* (both of which, especially the former, are most rewarding) make it plain that he would have been both hurt and indignant at any suggestion that he was perhaps not really 'Scottish' as a *man*. Forthright upholder of the Union though he was, he nonetheless voices again and again his personal exasperation or sorrow at this or that slight to which he feels Scotland is being subjected by the London-based government.

As a person Scott eludes anything like classification. No doubt that must be true of any considerable writer, but Scott's complexities are particularly extreme. He was an astonishingly industrious author, yet, if one is to believe all he said, he looked somewhat askance at the profession of letters and attached more importance to his adventures in the world of business and property. He was a staunch supporter of government and Crown, yet at the same time nostalgic for the old pre-Union Scotland he was born too late to have known.

Such a man, whose make-up was a remarkable mixture of the profoundly conservative with the self-consciously progressive, can be most irritating to the reader who wants simple formulae, who sees what the fashion of today calls 'commitment' as the highest virtue. To that kind of reader Scott will appear to be a sitter-on-the-fence, a prevaricator, or, to use that most solemn word of modern abuse, a 'liberal'. I hope to show that he certainly does not sit on the fence, and that if he can worthily be called liberal for the breadth of his sympathies he is far from being, in any intelligent sense, non-committed.

No book gives more challenging an impression of the characteristic Scott than *Waverley*, his first novel. It begins, indeed, to have its effect upon us as soon as we ask the preliminary question: just what is it 'about'? On the most obvious level it concerns the Jacobite Rebellion of 1745, that at once desperate and heroic

11

attempt to put the House of Stuart back on the British throne in place of the House of Hanover. It was the climax of a resentment dating back to 1688, when James II of England (who was at the same time James VII of Scotland, the two thrones having been united before the actual political Union between the two countries) was deposed in favour of William of Orange: a resentment felt most strongly by the Scottish Highlanders, but shared by numerous Lowland gentry, and by many, too, of the old nobility of England. The conflict was not simply one of allegiances to different royal houses, but existed between Tory and Whig, and between adherents of the Roman Catholic Church and the various kinds of Protestantism that had established their hold during the seventeenth century.

But *Waverley* is not a book whose purpose is to give us chunks of history thinly disguised as fiction. Scott's design is not the teaching of history without tears. True, the character who gives the novel its title belongs to a family noted for its loyalty to the Stuarts; he is an unwitting eyewitness of the gathering of Highlanders for the Rebellion, an event which he believes to be merely a stag-hunt; he finds himself at first involuntarily associated with the rebels, then swept off his feet by the attractive figure of Prince Charles Edward, son of the exiled James, the 'Bonnie Prince Charlie' of song and story and leader of the adventure. There are accounts of two battles, and Waverley is ultimately extricated from an involvement which he had never proposed to himself on his first going to Scotland. All this, however, hardly amounts to saying that Scott has offered a 'history' of the Rebellion. The ' '45', as it is still called, is not there in the book for its own sake, with the various characters used simply to dress up historical fact.

The truth is that the events of the '45 gave Scott a vehicle for exploring interests that were central for him, central for an intelligent and widely-read Scotsman whose lifetime bridged the eighteenth and nineteenth centuries. I group those interests under two very broad heads, the Romantic and the Heroic, though the separation has been adopted purely for convenience in discussion. It should soon become clear that the two heads cannot really be seen as distinct from each other. But with that qualification in mind let us consider what the notion of the Romantic means in this novel.

To start with, there is Scott's own place in what we call the Romantic Movement. I offer no set definition of Romanticism, but we may agree that Scott shares certain fairly conspicuous characteristics with other major writers thought of as belonging to the movement. There is, for instance, his liking for wild scenery (the setting Flora Mac-Ivor chooses for her recital of Gaelic verses in Chapter 22 is a case in point), which links him with Wordsworth, Coleridge, Shelley, and the Byron of *Childe Harold*. Then his predilection for the supernatural, or sometimes just strong hints of the supernatural, connects him with the best-selling Romanticism of the so-called Tales of Terror, those precursors of the modern thriller, the novels of Mrs Radcliffe above all. In *Waverley* this element appears in Fergus Mac-Ivor's visions of the 'Bodach Glas', a traditional family spectre. Also related to the Tales of Terror, and to much of Byron, is a type of male character who may be roughly described as the 'hero–villain': a type in whom the proportion of good to evil, fair to threatening, varies from one specific example to another, but who always seems either to live under a curse or to be driven by an alarming obsessive energy, or both. Though other Scott novels contain clearer instances of the type (some, indeed, are excessively clear), Fergus Mac-Ivor is to some extent a subtle variant. Finally in this rough conspectus there is that attachment to the rural, the homespun, the traditional, which Scott shares with both Wordsworth and the Coleridge of *The Rime of the Ancient Mariner*.

But there is one thing Scott, in his imaginative work as distinct from his letters and *Journal*, does *not* have in common with most of the great Romantic figures: their concern with overtly *personal* emotion. He is not his own hero, as Wordsworth and Shelley, in very different ways, are respectively the heroes of *The Prelude* and the *Ode to the West Wind*. Of course all the Romantics wrote a deal of poetry that is far less self-directed, but it will hardly be denied that a preoccupation with emotion intensely personal to the author is a striking characteristic of the movement. Yet Scott, seemingly one of Romanticism's leading figures and certainly a most influential one, is quite without it.

This would suggest that in a major respect he is set apart from Romanticism in general. Indeed, it is tempting to join some modern enthusiasts in asserting that he is fundamentally anti-Romantic, explaining away most of the shared characteristics I have noted (though not the interest in the traditional) by the argument that he had to include such things to win a large popular audience. Yet to rush without large qualification to so extreme a view does not aid understanding of so complex a make-up as his. He was undoubtedly well aware of his audience, for he wanted to make money, but the prevalence of evidently Romantic elements in his work is too striking to be written off in all its manifestations merely as concession to popular taste. As for his being positively anti-Romantic, there is no major figure of the movement, with the possible exception of Shelley, of whom this could not be said, if one wished, with regard to some of his work – which is a good reason for only using the term 'Romantic' broadly, without aiming for definition.

Instead of trying to see Scott as a crusader against Romanticism, then, let us consider the Romantic in *Waverley*, with two questions kept particularly in mind. Firstly, if Scott often appears to be anti-Romantic, to what extent and in what sense is it really true? Secondly, if we discount the argument of concession to popular taste, do the evidently Romantic things in the book have a definite function?

There certainly is warrant for supposing this novel to be a kind of fictional sermon against Romanticism as an influence upon the individual life. Here the account in the early chapters of Edward Waverley's boyhood and his attitude towards learning has an evident importance, for Scott will later wish us to understand that the adult Waverley is what his education has made him. Take this, from Chapter 3:

His powers of apprehension were so uncommonly quick as almost to resemble intuition, and the chief care of his preceptor was to prevent him, as a sportsman would phrase it, from overrunning his game – that is, from acquiring his knowledge in a slight, flimsy, and inadequate manner. And here the instructor had to combat another propensity too often united with brilliancy of fancy and vivacity of talent – that indolence, namely, of disposition, which can only be stirred by some strong motive of gratification, and which renounces study as soon as curiosity is gratified, the pleasure of conquering the first difficulties exhausted, and the novelty of pursuit is at an end. Edward would throw himself with spirit upon any classical author of which his preceptor proposed the perusal, make himself master of the style so far as to understand the story, and, if that pleased or interested him, he finished the volume. But it was in vain to attempt fixing his attention on critical distinctions of philology, upon the difference of idiom, the beauty of felicitous expression, or the artificial combinations of syntax. 'I can read and understand a Latin author,' said young Edward, with the self-confidence and rash reasoning of fifteen, 'and Scaliger or Bentley could not do much more.' Alas! while he was thus permitted to read only for the gratification of his amusement, he foresaw not that he was losing for ever the opportunity of acquiring habits of firm and assiduous application, of gaining the art of controlling, directing, and concentrating the powers of his mind for earnest investigation – an art far more essential than even that intimate acquaintance with classical learning which is the primary object of study. (14)

Only readers approaching the book as mainly an historical chronicle could agree with those who think such passages tiresomely unnecessary. As will be seen later, Scott does have an interest in the '45 which we can, in a special sense, call 'historical'; but in this book he is neither a painstaking assembler of documentation nor a purveyor of the modern historical bestseller's 'background colour'. One of his cardinal preoccupations, indeed, is more properly described as psychological: a preoccupation with the seductive appeal of the Stuart cause for such a person as Waverley, whose impressionable nature is so much the product of early habits. Yet, despite his weaknesses, Waverley cannot be seen as condemned with a harsh austerity in the passage just quoted. Scott may shake his head at opportunities lost, he may regret that Waverley was intellectually so undisciplined, but there is more than a touch of sympathy for the teenager who disregards 'critical distinctions of philology' and 'the artifical combinations of syntax' in favour of the straight question 'Does the book I am reading interest me or not?' If Scott is asking us to look at him critically, he is not inviting us to be too gravely censorious.

Chapter 4, which continues the story of Waverley's formation, introduces us to his ardently romantic predilections. (The word 'romantic' will be printed without a capital when its reference is to individual disposition, while the form 'Romantic' will be used for references specifically literary or artistic.) Not only does reading play acutely upon his sensibility; he can be roused by conjuring up visions of stirring, picturesque, or pathetic events in his own family's past. Here, for instance, we find him day-dreaming about the dramatic return home of Wilibert of Waverley:

In the corner of the large and sombre library, with no other light than was afforded by the decaying brands on its ponderous and ample hearth, he would exercise for hours that internal sorcery by which past or imaginary events are presented in action, as it were, to the eye of the muser. Then arose in long and fair array the splendour of the bridal feast at Waverley Castle; the tall and emaciated form of its real lord, as he stood in his pilgrim's weeds, an unnoticed spectator of the festivities of his supposed heir and intended bride; the electrical shock occasioned by the discovery; the springing of the vassals to arms; the astonishment of the bridegroom; the terror and confusion of the bride; the agony with which Wilibert observed that her heart as well as consent was in these nuptials; the air of dignity, yet of deep feeling, with which he flung down the half-drawn sword, and turned away for ever from the house of his ancestors.   (21)

That passage is of special interest. For besides being part of the laying bare of Waverley's romantic disposition, the disposition that will make him impulsively pledge himself to Prince Charles Edward, it is also extremely personal to the author, Walter Scott.

Now that may seem to contradict what I said about the absence in Scott of the overtly personal. Actually there is no contradiction. Edward Waverley is not the novelist in disguise. Here, as elsewhere in his work, Scott is not his own hero. But in the character of Waverley, and in the whole working-out of the book, he is investigating problems and tensions which were acutely his, dramatizing them through a fictional hero and the circumstances in which he is placed rather than giving them directly personal expression. Instead of saying 'I, Walter Scott, have a basically romantic disposition, and often feel uncomfortable about it, little as I care to give it up', he explores the matter in terms of a character very different from himself. At least, Waverley is quite different from Scott the man as regards weaker personality traits, though the latter's adventures in business and property, pursued with rash exuberance, might strike us, however unromantic they sound in themselves, as expressing a spirit not wholly unlike that which leads his hero into joining an armed rebellion.

But that is to stray into biography, intriguing as it is. What most relevantly emerges from our passage is something which links up with one side of Scott as a *novelist*; for he is here analysing, in terms of the fictitious Edward Waverley, that predilection for evoking the past for its own picturesque sake which was later to produce what I called in the first chapter the 'historical fantasias'. The imagined return of Wilibert of Waverley is exactly the kind of event upon which the big 'scenes' of those novels are often based. Yet here, in his very first novel, Scott is looking at that predilection for history embodied in the obviously colourful and dramatic with definitely critical eyes. He does not castigate Waverley so as to alienate the reader's sympathy, but his critical position is clear from the heading of Chapter 4: 'Castle-Building'. And consider, moreover, the words which end the chapter:

> Through these scenes it was that Edward loved to 'chew the cud of sweet and bitter fancy', and, like a child among his toys, culled and arranged, from the splendid yet useless imagery and emblems with which his imagination was stored, visions as brilliant and as fading as those of an evening sky. The effect of this indulgence upon his temper and character will appear in the next chapter. (22)

The romantic propensity is there seen as both childish and futile, as the manifestation of a prolonged and potentially damaging immaturity.

Scott's attitude has more to it than that judgement alone, however, for the critically observed propensity, even at this stage of his career, is a very real part of the author's make-up. To look at something critically is not to say that in all its manifestations one altogether despises it. The very fact that so much of Scott's later, if far less interesting, work drew largely upon the 'Castle-Building' vein proves that he did not write it off. What seems to have happened is that he came to exploit the vein more or less uncritically. It was popular, it paid dividends. To that extent those who argue that he was guided by the market in his use of Romantic material are justified. But they are not right in supposing that he was ever merely cynical in using it, or that in a book like *Waverley* it figures as a sop to popular taste.

The position may be suggested as follows: *Waverley* is the work of a writer deeply attracted by the wild, the picturesque, the stirring, yet who is at the same time acutely suspicious of their charms; a man who believes that the individual unduly swayed by them will at best be incomplete and at worst court sheer disaster. Scott is both Romantic *and* anti-Romantic. He is at once a Romantic at heart, and a vigilant critic of his own Romanticism.

How is this explored in the later treatment of Waverley, when he has made the fateful journey to Scotland that will embroil him in armed conspiracy? It comes out first of all in his disposition to find romance in almost everything. In Chapter 8, for instance, we follow him through the parks of Tully-Veolan, whose 'solitude and repose' seem to him 'almost monastic', and when he reaches the court of the Baron of Bradwardine's house we feel that he is, so to speak, imposing his own 'atmosphere' upon the place: 'Everything around appeared solitary, and would have been silent, but for the continued plashing of the fountain; and the whole scene still maintained the monastic illusion which the fancy of Waverley had conjured up.' A faintly comic light is cast on that by the mundane practicality of the immediately preceding sentence: 'The court was spacious, well paved, and perfectly clean, there being probably another entrance behind the stables for removing the litter.'

Seeking the master of the house at the beginning of the next chapter, he almost imagines himself to be in a world of legendary fancy, 'Filled almost with expectation of beholding some "old old man, with beard as white as snow"', whom he might question concerning this deserted mansion...' Again there is a somewhat absurd contrast between Waverley's feelings and the actuality of the place, for there follows a description of the highly artificially and formally laid out garden, decidedly at odds with any idea of unfrequented desolation. All the same, Scott's emphasis upon the garden's orderliness, which seems to belong to a world of sobriety and reason, is most interestingly qualified by the observation of genuinely wild and untamed features adjacent to it:

The garden, which seemed to be kept with great accuracy, abounded in fruit-trees, and exhibited a profusion of flowers and evergreens cut into grotesque forms. It was laid out in terraces, which descended rank by rank from the western wall to a large brook, which had a tranquil and smooth appearance where it served as a boundary to the garden; but, near the extremity, leapt in tumult over a strong dam, or wear-head, the cause of its temporary tranquillity, and there forming a cascade, was overlooked by an octagonal summerhouse, with a gilded bear on top by way of vane. After this feat, the brook, assuming its natural rapid and fierce character, escaped from the eye down a deep and wooded dell, from the copse of which arose a massive, but ruinous tower, the former habitation of the Barons of Bradwardine. (47)

wear-head weir-head

It is as though Scott were telling us not to laugh at Waverley too easily, reminding us that sobriety and reason can live very close to wildness and romance – sometimes most unexpectedly close.

For all that, Waverley's reactions to Tully-Veolan have a deal of comedy in them when one considers the people he meets there. He finds something 'bordering on the romantic' in what he gleans about the history of David Gellatley, an apparently lunatic retainer, but there is little romance about that personage himself, with his slily appropriate songs. Still less can romance be thought of in connection with Bailie Macwheeble, or the visitors Balmawhapple and Killancureit, or the drunken goings-on which result in a duel between Balmawhapple and the baron. As for the baron himself, he is markedly different from his Highland allies in the Rebellion in being quite scornful of superstitition. Moreover he stands in evidently total antithesis to Waverley in his attitudes towards literature and history. We learn in Chapter 13 that, whereas 'Edward...loved to fill up and round the sketch with the colouring of a warm and vivid imagination', the baron 'only cumbered his memory with matters of fact – the cold, dry, hard outlines which history delineates'.

I shall return to the baron later in this chapter, but it may be suggested in advance that 'cold', 'dry', and 'hard', though the words point to his intellectual cast with fair accuracy, do not tell us the whole truth about the man. We have already noted one passage in which the formality of his garden is set beside something far more rugged. Here is another, a description of the view from Rose Bradwardine's balcony:

The formal garden, with its high bounding walls, lay below, contracted, as it seemed, to a mere parterre; while the view extended beyond them down a wooded glen, where the small river was sometimes visible, sometimes hidden in copse. The eye might be delayed by a desire to rest on the rocks, which here and there rose from the dell with massive or spiry fronts, or it might dwell on the noble, though ruined tower, which was here beheld in all its dignity, frowning from a promontory over the river. (76)

Scott does not offer so striking a juxtaposition of dissimilarities as we find in Coleridge's *Kubla Khan*, yet his passage has an effect not wholly unlike these lines from that poem:

> So twice five miles of fertile ground
> With walls and towers were girdled round:
> And there were gardens bright with sinuous rills,
> Where blossomed many an incense-bearing tree;
> And here were forests ancient as the hills,
> Enfolding sunny spots of greenery.
>
> But oh! that deep romantic chasm which slanted
> Down the green hill athwart a cedarn cover!
> A savage place! as holy and enchanted
> As e'er beneath a waning moon was haunted
> By woman wailing for her demon-lover!

In both there is a contrast between the formally ordered and the primitively wild, the two elements co-existing in the one overall landscape. Does their co-existence in the setting of the baron's home symbolically hint, therefore, at a greater complexity in him than his severe rationality and erudite pedantry would lead us to expect? Might he perhaps turn out to be a kind of romantic himself, of maybe an even deeper hue than Edward Waverley? It is too early in our discussion to attempt an answer, but the matter is worth raising here as evidence of the kind of question this sophisticated novel makes the reader ask. No simple-minded Romantic author (and some hostile critics have seen Scott as just that) could allow so apparently unlikely a query to be put.

To resume consideration of the book's isolatably anti-Romantic features, however, there is the course of its love-interest. It could at first seem that nothing could be more insipidly ordinary than Waverley's unrequited passion for Flora Mac-Ivor: a view which would be quite justified were he shown as permanently cut to the heart by her rejection of him and Byronically doom-ridden ever after. In fact Waverley simply falls out of love with Flora, a sadly un-Romantic thing to do. Her studied coldness at Edinburgh, during the short-lived Court of Charles Edward, has the very effect she desires, while Waverley comes to see more and more in the Rose Bradwardine he has earlier regarded as doubtless charming but uncaptivating to a person of his sensibility. Consider how he views Rose in Chapter 14:

> She was too frank, too confiding, too kind; amiable qualities, undoubtedly, but destructive of the marvellous, with which a youth of imagination delights to address the empress of his affections. Was it possible to bow, to tremble, and to adore, before the timid, yet playful little girl, who now asked Edward to mend her pen, now to construe a stanza in Tasso, and now how to spell a very – very long word in her version of it? All these incidents have their fascination on the mind at a certain period of life, but not when a youth is entering it, and rather looking out for some object whose affection may dignify him in his own eyes than stooping to one who looks up to him for such distinction. (85)

The key phrase there is 'at a certain period in life'. If Waverley comes to view Rose quite differently later on, it is because he can then see her as she is, and see Flora, likewise, as *she* is; whereas in the early stage he judges them according to the extent to which they fit in with his daydream of what a romantic passion should be like. By the end of the book he has in important respects, and in a very short time, moved from one 'period in life' to another.

One decidedly un-Romantic feature of the love story, of course, is the approving way in which Fergus Mac-Ivor looks upon Waverley's feeling for Flora. He does have some genuine fondness for Waverley, but more than any tender support for success in love is his desire to see Flora mistress of Waverley-Honour, Edward's ancestral home. For Fergus, Waverley is primarily a grand social and economic and therefore political 'catch'.

But just as those passages concerned with the garden at Tully-Veolan suggest a warning that we should not stress the book's anti-Romanticism unremittingly, so the circumstances in which Waverley falls in love with Flora awaken quite complex reactions. In Chapter 22, when Waverley has begun what he supposes will be a short visit to Fergus Mac-Ivor, undertaken to penetrate beyond 'the dusky barrier of mountains', a source of romantic curiosity during his stay with his own uncle's 'ancient friend' the baron, Flora indulges him with a recital of Gaelic verses, which she is pleased to render in an English version. Without the slightest intent to captivate him personally, she deliberately chooses a spot that she feels will heighten the effect of the verses themselves. As she puts it to him, 'To speak in the poetical language of my country, the seat of the Celtic muse is in the mist of the secret and solitary hill, and her voice in the murmur of the mountain stream.' Accordingly she instructs an attendant girl to lead Waverley to the chosen *mise-en-scène*:

At a short turning the path, which had for some furlongs lost sight of the brook, suddenly placed Waverley in front of a romantic waterfall. It was not so remarkable either for great height or quantity of water as for the beautiful accompaniments which made the spot interesting. After a broken cataract of about twenty feet, the stream was received in a large natural basin filled to the brim with water, which, when the bubbles of the fall subsided, was so exquisitely clear that, although it was of great depth, the eye could discern each pebble at the bottom. Eddying round this reservoir, the brook found its way over a broken part of the ledge, and formed a second fall, which seemed to seek the very abyss; then, wheeling out beneath from among the smooth dark rocks which it had polished for ages, it wandered murmuring down the glen, forming the stream up which Waverley had just ascended. The borders of this romantic reservoir corresponded in beauty; but it was beauty of a stern and commanding cast, as if in the act of expanding into grandeur. Mossy banks of turf were broken and interrupted by huge fragments of rock, and decorated with trees and shrubs, some of which had been planted under the direction of Flora, but so cautiously that they added to the grace without diminishing the romantic wildness of the scene. (138)

That passage has no flavour of satire at the expense of the 'romantic', a word which candidly figures three times, without the slightest hint of irony. Nothing implies a suggestion that you are rather weak-minded if you like this kind of thing; for, although the landscape is seen from Waverley's point of view, Scott's own enjoyment in describing it is patent. On the other hand, one could hardly accuse the passage of heavily awe-inspiring 'sublimity'. Scott does not give the waterfall over-grandiose dimensions, and while the 'stern and commanding cast' of the surroundings is observed, he does not exaggerate its impressiveness. Their beauty is caught, so to speak, 'in the act of expanding into grandeur', instead of being given the more obvious and facile attribute of grandeur itself. The passage exhibits, indeed, a care and control (consider the way in which the appropriately tortuous course of the prose suggests the course of the brook) which might prompt the comment that if this is Romanticism, as in a sense it plainly is, it is Romanticism as clear in the head as the water in the 'romantic reservoir'.

In the next paragraph, though, something of a change sets in. A good deal has to do with the appearance of the verb 'to decorate' in two adjacent sentences, one of them at the end of the last quotation, the second coming as the new paragraph opens:

Here, like one of those lovely forms which decorate the landscapes of Poussin, Waverley found Flora gazing on the waterfall. Two paces further back stood Cathleen, holding a small Scottish harp, the use of which had been taught to Flora by Rory Dall, one of the last harpers of the Western Highlands. The sun, now stooping in the west, gave a rich and varied tinge to all the objects which surrounded Waverley, and seemed to add more than human brilliancy to the full expressive darkness of Flora's eye, exalted the richness and purity of her complexion, and enhanced the dignity and grace of her beautiful form. Edward thought he had never, even in his wildest dreams, imagined a figure of such exquisite and interesting loveliness. The wild beauty of the retreat, bursting upon him as if by magic, augmented the mingled feeling of delight and awe with which he approached her, like a fair enchantress of Boiardo or Ariosto, by whose nod the scenery around seemed to have been created an Eden in the wilderness. (138)

Of Flora's discreet gardening I shall say something when I have looked at the whole passage. What strikes one first of all with the repetition of the idea of *decoration* is the entry of a new note: a note of artificiality. Nothing till now has suggested the quality of a stylized landscape, yet at this point we are suddenly reminded of one of the most conscious 'arrangers' of landscape who ever painted – the seventeenth-century French artist Poussin. Consider, too, the way in which Flora appears at the end of the paragraph: 'like a fair enchantress of Boiardo or Ariosto'. No real sister of a fiercely calculating if sophisticated Highland chieftain, but an apparition out of Renaissance literature. And all this reflects the mind of Waverley. Responsive as he is to the natural beauty of the scene, his disposition is to take it out of the here and now, and translate it into terms of painting and poetry.

If the reader is invited to enjoy the scene evoked in the previous paragraph, and to agree that it *is* 'romantic' without a sense that the author is condescending to a taste for the picturesque that he does not really share, Waverley's reactions, on the other hand, come over to us as more than a little absurd. And there is a further reason for suspecting amusement on Scott's part. Without claiming that he is offering straight parody, one can quite easily see a link between the apparition of Flora in such a setting and the stage-properties of the type of sentimental novel ridiculed in Chapter I: the tale which has 'a heroine with a profusion of auburn hair, and a harp, the soft solace of her solitary hours, which she fortunately finds always the means of transporting from castle to cottage'. Flora does not have auburn hair, and her harp is small enough to be non-miraculously transported, but there is just enough reminiscence of sentimental novelistic cliché (the stock-in-trade of the more inferior brands of early Romanticism) to afford a humorous contrast with the real and quite unsentimental reason for Flora's appearing in such a scene. Not by some remarkable vicissitude of extravagant adventure is she found there, but according to her own deliberate plan, and she is realistic enough to know that she will create an effect, even though she does not bargain for its nature:

Flora, like every beautiful woman, was conscious of her own power, and pleased with its effects, which she could easily discern from the respectful yet confused address of the young soldier. But, as she possessed excellent sense, she gave the romance of the scene and other accidental circumstances full weight in appreciating the feelings with which Waverley seemed obviously to be impressed; and, unacquainted with the fanciful and susceptible peculiarities of his character, considered his homage as the passing tribute which a woman of even inferior charms might have expected in such a situation.

(138-9)

Flora emerges here as one who in her own way is certainly 'susceptible' to the beauty of the place, but who at the same time possesses a quite toughly pragmatic mentality. Thus her 'exquisite and interesting loveliness', though we are meant to take it as real, not just a delusion of the enchanted Waverley, has behind it a sober rationality far removed from her admirer's extravagance. Flora may be, as I shall argue later, truly a 'romantic' in a profound sense. Here, however, the way in which she consciously *uses* her own beauty and its setting, albeit with innocent purpose, indicates a disposition at odds with temperamental romanticism of the Waverley type.

Now we can see the point of that sentence about her subdued adornment of the landscape: 'Mossy banks of turf were broken and interrupted by huge fragments of rock, and decorated with trees and shrubs, some of which had been planted under the direction of Flora, but so cautiously that they added to the grace without diminishing the romantic wildness of the scene.' The impression is opposite in effect to that given by the descriptions of the baron's garden. Instead of cultivated formality qualified by adjacent natural ruggedness, we now have the hand of cultivation, deliberate though discreet, introducing hints of nurture into the midst of the really wild. And when we look back on this from later in the book we see its symbolic aptness. We, and Waverley with us, come to realize that Flora's 'exquisite and interesting loveliness' belongs to a person whose fanatical dedication to the Stuart cause is indeed, like the landscape, 'of a stern and commanding cast, as if in the act of expanding into grandeur', yet qualified by her possession of an essentially cool, orderly, and steady mind. One normally thinks of any fanaticism as being by definition an irrational affair, but Flora Mac-Ivor can paradoxically speak in a coolly rational way about her own irrationality, when, in Chapter 27, she firmly though gently rejects Waverley's advances. Her decorative landscaping, then, while far too cautious to suggest a thoroughgoing stylization and architectural formality, does symbolically parallel that lucid orderliness of mind co-existing so oddly with the obsession with the Stuart cause which she admits to have been hers since infancy.

The whole long passage thus affects the reader in sharply contrasting but rapidly successive and even simultaneous ways. There are genuine enjoyment of the setting, touches of ironic comedy, and important evidence, both literal and symbolic, regarding Flora's cast of mind. If she cannot be simply dubbed 'romantic' or 'anti-romantic', the same has to be said of the total effect, whose mixed quality is maintained to the end of the chapter.

Flora's verses, though they may not strike us as distinguished poetry, are offered by Scott as owning both the serious interest and the Romantic thrill of Highland tradition, while the element of partly deflating comedy reappears with the interruption of the song by Fergus's dog, not to mention Flora's rather sardonic résumé of the stanzas she will consequently not have time to sing. Though she is very far from mocking their content, for her irony is really directed against the shortcomings of her translation, the relaxed lightness of her tone counters too solemn an attitude towards bardic inspirations. Moreover the next chapter opens with Fergus and his sister exchanging jests about poetic conventions; not, as might at first be felt, an unacceptable incongruity in such a setting, but a reminder that while Fergus is a Highland chieftain, he is also partly a product of French sophisticated culture, his father having fled to France after the failure of an attempt to reinstate the Stuarts in 1715. And that in turn reminds us of the extraordinarily contrasting main sources of the '45: wild mountains and a polished Court, fierce feudalism and French metropolitan urbanity. That in itself points to this novel's mingling of the more obviously Romantic with apparently antithetical strains. The mixture is inherent in the very circumstances of the Rebellion.

One kind of mixture to be found in *Waverley* is a combination of ironic comedy with the grimly serious. Consider what Rose Bradwardine tells Edward in Chapter 15 about relations between Fergus and her father (we find them first in a state of conflict, before their renewed friendship and alliance in the Rebellion) and the type of unhappy situation that has arisen in the past:

'Dear Captain Waverley, try your influence with my father to make matters up. I am sure this is but the beginning of our troubles; for Tully-Veolan has never been a safe or quiet residence when we have been at feud with the Highlanders. When I was a girl about ten, there was a skirmish fought between a party of twenty of them and my father and his servants behind the mains; and the bullets broke several panes in the north windows, they were so near. Three of the Highlanders were killed, and they brought them in wrapped in their plaids, and laid them on the stone floor of the hall; and next morning, their wives and daughters came, clapping their hands, and crying the coronach, and shrieking, and carried away the dead bodies, with the pipes playing before them. I could not sleep for six weeks without starting and thinking I heard these terrible cries, and saw the bodies lying on the steps, all stiff and swathed up in their bloody tartans.' (92)

mains farmhouse; *coronach* lament

For Rose there is nothing of romance in all this; it is just dangerous and horribly worrying. But Waverley views it differently:

Waverley could not help starting at a story which bore so much resemblance to one of his own day-dreams. Here was a girl scarce seventeen, the gentlest of her sex, both in temper and appearance, who had witnessed with her own eyes such a scene as he had used to conjure up in his imagination, as only occurring in ancient times, and spoke of it coolly, as one very likely to recur. He felt at once the impulse of curiosity, and that slight sense of danger which only serves to heighten its interest. He might have said with Malvolio, 'I do not now fool myself, to let imagination jade me! I am actually in the land of military and romantic adventures, and it only remains to be seen what will be my own share in them.' (92)

That is a key passage, for out of it comes the whole subsequent development of Waverley's *real* 'education', as opposed to the 'Castle-Building' that early habits have encouraged. Scott here suggests the mixture of comedy and grimness which will ensue, for if the reference to the Malvolio of *Twelfth Night* indicates that Waverley will in some way be made a fool of, the phrase '*military* and *romantic* adventures' points to his eventual realization that the military and the romantic are by no means necessarily to be equated with each other, but are more often than not at ghastly variance.

I shall take three examples of ways in which the ideas so far thrown out are taken up and developed. On the more comic side there is the beginning of Chapter 16, where first we find the baron learnedly holding forth on Highland custom and culture. Pedantic as his exposition is, Waverley's romantic susceptibilities are excited by all this talk of what is to him the rich and strange: 'Edward's curiosity became highly interested, and he inquired whether it was possible to make with safety an excursion into the neighbouring Highlands, whose dusky barrier of mountains had already excited his wish to penetrate beyond them.' Note that qualifying phrase, 'with safety'. Waverley's romanticism is at this stage still of a carefully prudential nature. This gives a comic flavour to what follows, for as the baron goes on to assure him that his wishes can certainly be met, Edward receives a shock:

While they were on this topic, the door suddenly opened, and, ushered by Saunders Saunderson, a Highlander, fully armed and equipped, entered the apartment. Had it not been that Saunders acted the part of master of the ceremonies to this martial apparition, without appearing to deviate from his usual composure, and that neither Mr. Bradwardine nor Rose exhibited any emotion, Edward would certainly have thought the intrusion hostile. As it was, he started at the sight of what he had not yet happened to see, a mountaineer in his full national costume. (94–5)

In fact this young man, this 'apparition', Evan Dhu Maccombich, is the most utterly down-to-earth character in the book. The effect on Waverley of his seemingly dramatic entry and exotic appearance is a little blunted when he speaks to the baron in perfectly good English; or so Scott implies, especially when what most impresses Waverley subsequently in the chapter is not so much the air of the 'rich and strange' in Evan Dhu as 'the ingenuity he displayed in collecting information, and the precise and pointed conclusions which he drew from it'. The down-to-earthness of Evan Dhu persists to the end, and is responsible for one of the book's most tellingly mixed strokes. In Chapter 68, after the collapse of the Rebellion, Fergus and Evan are standing trial for high treason in the court at Carlisle. Fergus gives a defiant answer to the clerk's ritual question, '"What have you to say for yourselves why the Court should not pronounce judgment against you, that you die according to law?"' When Evan rises, however, his initial silence makes spectators suppose 'that the poor fellow intended to plead the influence of his superior as an excuse for his crime'. But when at last Evan speaks it is to very different purpose:

'I was only ganging to say, my lord,' said Evan, in what he meant to be an insinuating manner, 'that if your excellent honour and the honourable Court would let Vich Ian Vohr go free just this once, and let him gae back to France, and no to trouble King George's government again, that ony six o' the very best of his clan will be willing to be justified in his stead; and if you'll just let me gae down to Glennaquoich, I'll fetch them up to ye mysell, to head or hang, and you may begin wi' me the very first man.' (421)

ganging going; *gae* go; *ony* any

This proposal that six of Fergus's clansmen should suffer the death-penalty in their chieftain's stead certainly has a note of the grimly comic; but only from the point of view of the established legal system. Evan Dhu means it entirely seriously. To him such a contract would be both pragmatically business-like and fully in accord with traditional clan loyalty.

To return to Chapter 16, Waverley's romantic illusions, despite what turns out to be Evan Dhu's decidedly non-romantic reality, reach their height as he and his conductor wait by moonlight to be taken to 'The Hold of a Highland Robber' (heading of Chapter 17):

> He had now time to give himself up to the full romance of his situation. Here he sate on the banks of an unknown lake, under the guidance of a wild native, whose language was unknown to him, on a visit to the den of some renowned outlaw, a second Robin Hood, perhaps, or Adam o' Gordon, and that at deep midnight, through scenes of difficulty and toil, separated from his attendant, left by his guide. What a variety of incidents for the exercise of a romantic imagination, and all enhanced by the solemn feeling of uncertainty at least, if not of danger! The only circumstance which assorted ill with the rest was the cause of his journey – the Baron's milk-cows! This degrading incident he kept in the background. (100–1)

The comic touch at the end (for the baron's cows have in fact been at the centre of friction with the Highlanders) characteristically points the way to subsequent experiences. Donald Bean Lean, the Highland Robber himself, is anything but a picturesque romantic figure. An adroit manipulator and opportunist, he is squalid as well as dangerous, and comes to remind us, as do several other characters, of the dubious motives prevailing among too many apparent adherents to the Stuart cause. And when, in Chapter 18, Evan Dhu calmly voices the most heterodox assumptions regarding established legality in connection with such persons as Donald, Waverley's questions show him to be not a little uncomfortable. 'Romance is all very well, and I have a taste for it myself,' seems to be the implied comment that Scott is working towards; 'but let us have the kind of romance which is tolerably consonant with law and order. It's one thing to have a taste for wild scenery, and to be interested in the traditional and time-honoured. It's quite another to be drawn into intrigues that are desperate at best, and squalid at the worst. And if all that makes you laugh – well, there are many things a sensible man finds himself laughing at in this world.'

But *Waverley* is much more than a comic 'send-up' of immature romantic enthusiasm. I remarked on the ironic force of the phrase 'military and romantic adventures'. What happens to Edward when military operations really begin is that he finds romance turning into nightmare. After the stag-hunt in Chapter 24 he is 'gratified with the romantic effect' of the gathering and break-up of the 'various tribes assembled'. But it is another matter when the Rebellion, to which the stag-hunt is preparatory, actually starts *killing* people. Consider, far later in the book, Waverley's reactions to the deaths of Houghton and Colonel Gardiner, both of whom his involvement with the Rebellion has led him in different ways virtually to betray. Consider, too, his agony at the conviction that he has been responsible for the death of Colonel Talbot's child and for the dangerous illness of the mother. By then 'Castle-Building' has been well and truly abandoned. When in Chapter 63 Waverley returns to Scotland after his disentanglement from the now defeated rebels, in search of news of Rose and the baron, the drear aftermath of 'military and romantic adventures' confronts him on every side:

As he advanced northward, the traces of war became visible. Broken carriages, dead horses, unroofed cottages, trees felled for palisades, and bridges destroyed or only partially repaired – all indicated the movements of hostile armies. In those places where the gentry were attached to the Stuart cause, their houses seemed dismantled or deserted, the usual course of what may be called ornamental labour was totally interrupted, and the inhabitants were seen gliding about, with fear, sorrow, and dejection on their faces.

And there immediately follows the now inevitable comment on the course of Waverley's 'education':

It was evening when he approached the village of Tully-Veolan, with feelings and sentiments – how different from those which attended his first entrance! Then, life was so new to him that a dull or disagreeable day was one of the greatest misfortunes which his imagination anticipated, and it seemed to him that his time ought only to be consecrated to elegant or amusing study, and relieved by social or youthful frolic. Now, how changed! how saddened, yet how elevated was his character, within the course of a very few months! Danger and misfortune are rapid, though severe teachers. 'A sadder and a wiser man', he felt in internal confidence and mental dignity a compensation for the gay dreams which in his case experience had so rapidly dissolved.

(388)

Remote from one another as are their actual experiences, the educative discipline Waverley has undergone shows a parallel to the emotionally maturing processes gone through by Jane Austen's heroines in *Pride and Prejudice* and *Emma*.

Now, does all this mean that Scott's feeling about the romantic is that he approves of it in moderate doses but deplores it when it gets out of hand? That would be a cynical way of putting it, which will not really do, for the author's attitude is more serious and responsible. What we may say is that he shows us Waverley as having discovered the kind of reality which lies all too often behind glamorous trappings, *without*, however, turning him into a bitter cynic at an early age. If he has stopped 'Castle-Building', there is nothing in the late chapters to make us suppose him to have become emotionally dried-up. Rather the reverse, in fact. Growing away from the sillier side of personal romanticism does not have to mean emotional atrophy.

But here we must look at an obviously relevant passage, much used by modern commentators but not invariably understood for what it really represents. In Chapter 52 Flora gives Rose a compact sketch of Waverley's future as she sees it:

'I will tell you where he will be at home, my dear, and in his place – in the quiet circle of domestic happiness, lettered indolence, and elegant enjoyments of Waverley-Honour. And he will refit the old library in the most exquisite Gothic taste, and garnish its shelves with the rarest and most valuable volumes; and he will draw plans and landscapes, and write verses, and rear temples, and dig grottoes; and he will stand in a clear summer night in the colonnade before the hall, and gaze on the deer as they stray in the moonlight, or lie shadowed by the boughs of the huge old fantastic oaks; and he will repeat verses to his beautiful wife, who will hang upon his arm; – and he will be a happy man.' (328)

One can easily jump to the conclusion that the passage is simply a joke against both Waverley himself and the cult of the pseudo-Gothic in building and the pseudo-picturesque in landscape-gardening which gained ground in the mid- and later eighteenth century. To some extent that is justified. In a way Flora is dead right about Waverley. His notion of what is romantic has been

31

very much a matter of day-dreams in libraries. But is she being wholly fair? And are we as readers being wholly fair either, if we unquestioningly endorse her slightly contemptuous amusement as representing the view Scott wishes us to take?

I think not. Scott surely does expect us to be a little amused by the picture Flora draws, but, as in other places, there is qualification. After all, is it such a *thoroughly* contemptible future that she envisages for Waverley? Today it may be fashionable to think so, but Scott would hardly have been of that opinion himself. For although he could never in his life have been convicted of 'indolence', 'lettered' or otherwise, the picture is not wholly unlike that of the home he made for himself at Abbotsford. Seen from that point of view, the element of amusement is a manifestation of the self-irony one finds quite often in Scott, notably in *The Antiquary*. But a far more important question is whether it is possible truly to believe that Waverley, after his experiences in the Rebellion, can ever be the complacent dilettante sketched by Flora. One feels that his sense of what is 'comfortably' romantic (which is all she can associate with him) *must*, as his return to Tully-Veolan shows, be qualified by his experience of the non-romantic realities of war. Admittedly she is speaking before he has drained the full cup of bitter experience, but it is impossible to suppose that her attitude to him would ever have been different, given what she is.

For it is clear why Flora is one-sided, is only right up to a point. The reason is that if Waverley, until matured by grim chastening, is what might be called a 'parlour romantic', Flora is the real thing. In her absolutely unswerving devotion to the Stuart cause, utterly uncontaminated by any thought of personal advantage, she is truly a romantic, as Waverley can never be. She can be rational about her obsesssion, she can talk collectedly about it; but she can never put it aside. To restore the Stuarts to the throne – that is her romantic dream, and to it her whole life has been devoted. How different from the undirected day-dreaming of Waverley. In his treatment of Flora, Scott has the strength of the tragic realist. Tragic realism involves the individual who strives to live according to one objective, or ideal, or personal code, only to find that the pressures of real life make this out of the question. Given the ultimate impossibility, there is no further reason for existing. Flora does not die, but her retreat to a convent is as much a farewell to the world as her brother's execution.

If Scott cannot, then, be easily dubbed anti-Romantic in his treatment of Waverley, if what he castigates are the sillier and more superficial sides of Edward's outlook, can we say that he is being anti-Romantic in his handling of Flora? If Flora's romanticism is, as I have just said, the real thing, is it a 'real thing' of which he disapproves and invites the reader to disapprove? Again the question does not admit of an easy reply. Not only is Scott no lover of fanaticism; Flora herself, after the defeat of the rebels, feels hauntingly that her obsession has led to Fergus's death. Yet the consistently selfless purity of her devotion to the cause, though the author presents it as deplorable in its results, comes across to us as being in itself genuinely impressive.

This brings us to Scott's attitude towards the Rebellion as a whole, and to his treatment of the Heroic. But let us very briefly take stock, before passing to that second head. As far as the Romantic is concerned, it has been suggested that Scott can only with qualification be called anti-Romantic in his handling of Waverley. Those who overstress Scott's celebration of prose and reason overlook the fact that though the mild Rose Bradwardine replaces the tragic Flora in Edward's affections, his marriage is far from being just a matter of rational convenience. To speak truth, he is more 'in love' with Rose than he has ever been with Flora, for the earlier passion is an infatuation with a person really quite different from what he imagines her to be. In so far as Scott thus stresses the contrast between genuinely-founded feeling, as opposed to the passing figment, he is a Romantic indeed (in rather the same way as Jane Austen in *Persuasion*). Where Flora is concerned, Scott shows us a character Romantic in a far deeper, more disturbing sense, impressive as well as dangerous; and if the end of her story is tragic acceptance of reality, her devotion to an ideal objective is not in itself made to seem valueless. The treatment of her after the collapse of the '45 shows no rancour in the author. If he may not want such dangerous idealists around, he is nevertheless no man to sneer at them. As for the things he shares with other major Romantic writers, wild scenery is put to particular suggestive use in the surroundings of Tully-Veolan (of which more will shortly be said) and the setting Flora chooses for her Gaelic verses. While the landscapes are partly offered for their own attractiveness, they have a symbolic function going beyond that, like the mountains which romantically excite Waverley early on and which become the gate through which he enters the world of very non-romantic reality. I shall discuss the other shared Romantic characteristics when I come to look specifically at the role of Fergus.

It was said early in this chapter that *Waverley* does not properly permit separation of the Romantic from the Heroic. Clearly this is true in the case of Flora. Heroic striving toward the ideal goal is of a piece with her obsessive devotion. But distinctions and qualifications are once more to be observed. Consider a key passage from Chapter 21, where Flora's feeling about the Stuart cause is set beside that of her brother:

His looks seemed to seek glory, power, all that could exalt him above others in the race of humanity; while those of his sister, as if she were already conscious of mental superiority, seemed to pity, rather than envy, those who were struggling for any farther distinction. Her sentiments corresponded with the expression of her countenance. Early education had impressed upon her mind, as well as on that of the Chieftain, the most devoted attachment to the exiled family of Stuart. She believed it the duty of her brother, of his clan, of every man in Britain, at whatever personal hazard, to contribute to that restoration which the partizans of the Chevalier de St. George had not ceased to hope for. For this she was prepared to do all, to suffer all, to sacrifice all. But her loyalty, as it exceeded her brother's in fanaticism, excelled it also in purity. Accustomed to petty intrigue, and necessarily involved in a thousand paltry and selfish discussions, ambitious also by nature, his political faith was tinctured, at least, if not tainted, by the views of interest and advancement so easily combined with it; and at the moment he should unsheathe his claymore, it might be difficult to say whether it would be most with the view of making James Stuart a king or Fergus Mac-Ivor an earl. This, indeed, was a mixture of feeling which he did not avow even to himself, but it existed, nevertheless, in a powerful degree. (130)

The author's view of Fergus, we note, is a quite trenchantly critical one, and it extends beyond him to the Rebellion in general.

Fergus is not, of course, a Donald Bean Lean; nor does his behaviour when he awaits execution strike one as anything but
heroically dignified. Yet 'the views of interest and advancement',
more damagingly seen in other Jacobite supporters but still
integral to his nature, give the whole enterprise a lurking taint of
selfish expediency. To put it baldly, there is nothing Romantic
about *those* motives behind seemingly Heroic endeavour.

Here again, however, the reader must beware of rushing to extremes. If Scott views Fergus critically, it is most certainly not
with contempt. Nor does he seek to write off the Rebellion as
mere blustering folly. There is enough of the Edward Waverley
in him to make Scott see just how and why the desperate cause
was so attractive: attractive not primarily because of its more outwardly glamorous trappings, including the prince himself (who,
incidentally, is portrayed as an eminently politic manipulator of
Waverley's susceptibilities), but first and foremost because of
what it held of the very genuinely Heroic. For to the Highlanders the '45 was more than an attempt to restore a banished
royal house. It was the last effort to assert and preserve a way of
life, a cultural tradition, that was soon to be extinguished.

Scott is explicit about this side of the novel's interest in Chapter
72, 'A Postscript Which Should Have Been a Preface':

There is no European nation which, within the course of half a century or
little more, has undergone so complete a change as this kingdom of Scotland.
The effects of the insurrection of 1745, – the destruction of the patriarchal
power of the Highland chiefs, – the abolition of the heritable jurisdictions of
the Lowland nobility and barons, – the total eradication of the Jacobite party,
which, averse to mingle with the English, or adopt their customs, long
continued to pride themselves upon maintaining ancient Scottish manners
and customs, – commenced this innovation. The gradual influx of wealth and
extension of commerce have since united to render the present people of
Scotland a class of beings as different from their grandfathers as the existing
English are from those of Queen Elizabeth's time.

The political and economical effects of these changes have been traced by
Lord Selkirk with great precision and accuracy. But the change, though
steadily and rapidly progressive, has nevertheless been gradual; and, like
those who drift down the stream of a deep and smooth river, we are not aware
of the progress we have made until we fix our eye on the now distant point
from which we have been drifted. Such of the present generation as can
recollect the last twenty or twenty-five years of the eighteenth century will be

35

fully sensible of the truth of this statement; especially if their acquaintance and connexions lay among those who in my younger time were facetiously called 'folks of the old leaven', who still cherished a lingering, though hopeless, attachment to the house of Stuart.

This race has now almost entirely vanished from the land, and with it, doubtless, much absurd political prejudice; but also many living examples of singular and disinterested attachment to the principles of loyalty which they received from their fathers, and of old Scottish faith, hospitality, worth, and honour. (447–8)

Perhaps, indeed, it is wrong to see the Edward Waverley in Scott here, for the author's interest in the traditional is clearly far more that of the social historian than that of the Romantic story-teller. He knows that his account of Highland manners and customs will have a Romantic appeal, for their aura of there mote, rich and strange, and he feels a good deal of that sort of interest in them himself. But more central is his sense of commemorating that which had so rapidly passed away, and whose passing succeeded and completed by the Highland Clearances (which amounted to the destruction of the Highland society which had made the '45 possible), had left its scar on the Scotland of his own day and is certainly not forgotten in the Highlands of our modern age. It is this sense of processes going on in the Scotland in which he himself grew up (for the '45 was not many years behind), of the cruelty and waste involved, yet also of their inevitability, that makes Scott in a really important sense an 'historical' novelist, rather than the tinsel pageantry of *Ivanhoe*; makes him also, in an equally fundamental way, a 'Scottish' novelist, though his depiction of social change and detribalization has universal significance, not least in the developing countries of Asia and Africa today.

Critical Scott is, I have pointed out, of the self-advancing side of Fergus Mac-Ivor, not to mention characters who in more damaging respects make the '45 look sordid rather than Heroic; yet Fergus is impressively shown to us, despite his taste for intrigue, as the real focus of a living society. Here, indeed, rather than in military exploit or the short-lived colour of Charles Edward's Court, lies what can most fittingly be called Heroic in *Waverley*. For the sense we are given of an organically constituted Highland order, especially in Chapter 20, is that of a society from which epic can spring: not just because its members can be militantly explosive, but primarily because its homogeneity makes it powerfully aware of what its achievements have been, what its codes and traditions are – in a word, of what it culturally *is*. The reader is made very conscious of this when Mac-Murrough, 'the family *bhairdh*', gives his recital of Celtic verses:

He seemed to Edward, who attended him with much interest, to recite many proper names, to lament the dead, to apostrophise the absent, to exhort, and entreat, and animate those who were present. Waverley thought he even discerned his own name, and was convinced his conjecture was right from the eyes of the company being at that moment turned towards him simultaneously. The ardour of the poet appeared to communicate itself to the audience. Their wild and sunburnt countenances assumed a fiercer and more animated expression; all bent forward towards the reciter, many sprang up and waved their arms in ecstasy, and some laid their hands on their swords. When the song ceased, there was a deep pause, while the aroused feelings of the poet and of the hearers gradually subsided into their usual channel.   (127)

Doubtless the impact of things like that on the book's early readers was pre-eminently Romantic. While one now appreciates its function of showing that the clan has a 'voice', the manifestation of its corporate nature, the passage has its possibilities of absurdity. Scott is a very different writer from the Macpherson who produced that most notorious of literary hoaxes, the 'Ossian' poems, but the description of the *bhairdh*'s recital cannot help reminding us of the early Romantic thrill at the Celtic, real or fake.

The author is too sophisticated, however, not to anticipate such a reaction in the intelligent reader. Just as his seeming anti-Romanticism turns out to be a qualified affair, so his celebration of the Heroic, very real though it be, undergoes the restraining discipline of his lively and humorous mind. Take the very opening of Chapter 20, when Waverley has just arrived at Glennaquoich:

Ere Waverley entered the banqueting hall, he was offered the patriarchal refreshment of a bath for the feet, which the sultry weather, and the morasses he had traversed, rendered highly acceptable. He was not, indeed, so luxuriously attended upon this occasion as the heroic travellers in the Odyssey; the task of ablution and abstersion being performed, not by a beautiful damsel, trained

To chafe the limb, and pour the fragrant oil,

37

but by a smoke-dried skinny old Highland woman, who did not seem to think herself much honoured by the duty imposed upon her, but muttered between her teeth, 'Our fathers' herds did not feed so near together that I should do you this service.' A small donation, however, amply reconciled this ancient handmaiden to the supposed degradation; and, as Edward proceeded to the hall, she gave him her blessing in the Gaelic proverb, 'May the open hand be filled the fullest.' (124)

At first the effect seems largely satirical. Scott does not want us to think that he is over-solemnly pressing the Highlanders upon us as idealized Homeric figures. (There is a similarly deflating effect in Chapter 16, p. 98, when Evan Dhu, anxious to impress Waverley, takes aim at an eagle and misses.) The affair of the 'small donation' may in fact strike one as somewhat contemptuously anti-Heroic. But again what we have turns out to be other than a pure 'send-up'. For although the old woman, at a glance, appears venal in rather a pathetically familiar style, the proverb in which she goes on to bless Waverley obliges us to reflect that her interpretation of the gift is quite different from ours. To her it plainly figures not as a bribe, but as a symbolic substitute for orthodox ties (in her society's scale of values) which would make her perform the service without question. By his gift Edward has established what she now recognizes as a claim upon her. Thus the small incident, while retaining its anti-idealizing force, becomes at the same time part of the way in which conventions unfamiliar to modern European or Europeanized societies but authentic in their own contexts, are brought home to us by this book. Readers in many parts of Africa are likely to see Scott's point.

For the impressive organic solidity of a Highland community is what most comes across in this chapter: a community hierarchical and rigidly so, no doubt, yet still very much a composite whole even in the things which point to the stratification of men into *distinct* but not *separate* orders and functions:

At the head of the table was the Chief himself, with Edward, and two or three Highland visitors of neighbouring clans; the elders of his own tribe, wad-setters and tacksmen, as they were called, who occupied portions of his estate as mortgagers or lessees, sat next in rank; beneath them, their sons and nephews and foster-brethren; then the officers of the Chief's household, according to their order; and lowest of all, the tenants who actually cultivated the ground. Even beyond this long perspective, Edward might see upon the green, to which a huge pair of folding doors opened, a multitude of High-landers of a yet inferior description, who, nevertheless, were considered as guests, and had their share both of the countenance of the entertainer and of the cheer of the day. (124–5)

Fergus's clansmen accept this stratification, moreover, in all its inplications:

Excellent claret and champagne were liberally distributed among the Chief's immediate neighbours; whisky, plain or diluted, and strong beer refreshed those who sat near the lower end. Nor did this inequality of distribution appear to give the least offence. Every one present understood that his taste was to be formed according to the rank which he held at table; and, consequently, the tacksmen and their dependants always professed the wine was too cold for their stomachs, and called, apparently out of choice, for the liquor which was assigned to them from economy. (125)

Given the close-knit texture of that community, it comes as no surprise that Evan Dhu, many chapters later, should contemptu-ously spurn the judge who ventures some hope of his being spared execution. With his Chief dead, the centre of his world removed, Evan Dhu's life would no longer have any significance to him.

Yet, authentically Chief though Fergus monumentally is, we find even in Chapter 20 a tiny hint of qualification, a hint which suggestively links up with what we know of his mixed motives. After the account of the *bhairdh*'s song and its reception, comes the following:

The Chieftain, who, during this scene had appeared rather to watch the emotions which were excited than to partake their high tone of enthusiasm, filled with claret a small silver cup which stood by him. 'Give this,' he said to an attendant, 'to Mac-Murrough nan Fonn (*i.e.* of the songs), and when he has drunk the juice, bid him keep, for the sake of Vich Ian Vohr, the shell of the gourd which contained it.' The gift was received by Mac-Murrough with profound gratitude; he drank the wine, and, kissing the cup, shrouded it with reverence in the plaid which was folded on his bosom. (127)

While we are told that 'the clan regarded the generosity of their Chieftain with high approbation', it is hard not to suspect that he has been partly impelled to it by the desire to make the right kind of impression on Waverley. 'The politic Chieftain of the race of Ivor', as Scott calls Fergus when in Chapter 40 he introduces Edward to the prince, could hardly miss so expedient an occasion to please both his clan and the young Englishman he is anxious to enlist as political, military, and matrimonial ally. And although one does not find Fergus's chieftainly detachment during Mac-Murrough's song exactly odd or inappropriate to his status, or feel that the company observe anything unusual, one has the curious sense that one part of this man's make-up stands a little aside from it all – from the very community of which he is the focal point. Does the infusion of the courtly intriguer in the Highland Chieftain, one ponders, symbolically hint at a basic weakness in the '45 considered as an attempt to preserve a traditional order?

I remarked, when reviewing manifestly Romantic features of *Waverley*, that Fergus is to some extent a variant, a subtle one, on the type of the 'hero-villain'. He does not obviously belong to the category; he bears no mark of Cain, nor does he outwardly suggest the mien of 'the ruined archangel' (cf. next chapter, on *The Heart of Midlothian*). But he exhibits the characteristic blend of genuine grandeur with evilly frightening passion, as Waverley discovers, and if his clan has no hereditary curse, it has its hereditary spectre: the Bodach Glas, phantom of a man killed by an ancestor in a quarrel about division of booty. 'Since that time,' Fergus tells Edward in Chapter 59, 'his spirit has crossed the Vich Ian Vohr of the day when any great disaster was impending, but especially before approaching death.' Waverley, whose susceptibilities do not extend to belief in ghosts, has 'little doubt that this phantom was the operation of an exhausted frame and depressed spirits, working on the belief common to all Highlanders in such superstitions.' So, indeed, we may take it. This is not the only place in a Scott novel where the author induces the shudder of the supernatural and then goes on to suggest, or on some occasions simply to imply, a rational explanation. But here, although Fergus's tale of his meeting with the spectre is spine-chilling enough, the part played by the incident is by no means merely sensational. Here again Scott is not using the trappings of Romanticism for their own sake. For the real function of the incident, which occurs just as Fergus has shed the violent authoritarian aggressiveness towards Waverley that is his least admirable characteristic, is to remind us, simply and movingly, of his identity with his own people. In his absolute belief in what he has seen, and in the tradition behind it, Fergus is the Highlander, Vich Ian Vohr, rooted in the lore of 'the race of Ivor', and no longer the scheming politician. It is a fitting prelude to his dignified end.

Finally, what of the Baron of Bradwardine? He, of course, survives the Rebellion and its aftermath, yet he has been well and truly involved in the affair. At least, no one has been more staunch a champion of Charles Edward or more in evidence upon the field of battle. But one wonders, in spite of this, if his involvement is not of a slightly suspect kind. I am not suggesting that he suffers from anything approaching a taint of self-interest; rather that he embarks upon the enterprise, curiously enough, in the spirit of a special kind of personal romanticism. One begins to see the point of those mixed and mingled descriptions of his grounds. Symbolically they reveal the man. For alongside the baron's pedantic precision, his pompous erudition, his niggling over niceties, goes an attachment to the past *because* it is the past, which, despite the arcane learning surrounding it, must really be called romantic. Pedantry in his case is the expression of a bizarre kind of romanticism.

Scott at times rather overplays the baron's quaint erudition. A wildly idiosyncratic figure, he belongs to the category of Scott characters who anticipate Dickens. But Scott does not always know where to stop short in the parade of oddity, where Dickens usually does, with the result that Scott's figures can run the risk of boring. Some of the baron's learned outpourings could stand being halved in length. Here, though, consulting Fergus and Waverley, after the victorious battle of Prestonpans, about the way he can interpret ancient feudal law in rendering homage to Charles Edward, he is at his ridiculous best:

'I doubt na, lads,' he proceeded, 'but your education has been sae seen to that ye understand the true nature of the feudal tenures?'

Fergus, afraid of an endless dissertation, answered, 'Intimately, Baron,' and touched Waverley as a signal to express no ignorance.

'And ye are aware, I doubt not, that the holding of the barony of Bradwardine is of a nature alike honourable and peculiar, being blanch (which Craig opines ought to be Latinated *blancum*, or rather *francum*, a free holding) *pro servitio detrahendi, seu exuendi, caligas regis post battalliam.*' Here Fergus turned his falcon eye upon Edward, with an almost imperceptible rise of his

eyebrow, to which his shoulders corresponded in the same degree of eleva-
tion. 'Now, twa points of dubitation occur to me upon this topic. First,
whether this service, or feudal homage, be at any event due to the person of
the Prince, the words being, *per expressum, caligas REGIS*, the boots of the
king himself; and I pray your opinion anent that particular before we
proceed farther.'

'Why, he is Prince Regent,' answered Mac-Ivor, with laudable composure
of countenance; 'and in the court of France all the honours are rendered to
the person of the Regent which are due to that of the King. Besides, were I
to pull off either of their boots, I would render that service to the young
Chevalier ten times more willingly than to his father.'

'Ay, but I talk not of personal predilections. However, your authority is of
great weight as to the usages of the court of France: and doubtless the Prince,
as *alter ego*, may have a right to claim the *homagium* of the great tenants of the
crown, since all faithful subjects are commanded, in the commission of
regency, to respect him as the king's own person. Far, therefore, be it from
me to diminish the lustre of his authority by withholding this act of homage, so
peculiarly calculated to give it splendour; for I question if the Emperor of
Germany hath his boots taken off by a free baron of the empire. But here
lieth the second difficulty – the Prince wears no boots, but simply brogues and
trews.'

This last dilemma had almost disturbed Fergus's gravity.

'Why,' said he, 'you know, Baron, the proverb tells us, "It's ill taking the
breeks off a Highlandman," – and the boots are here in the same predicament.'

'The word *caligae*, however,' continued the Baron, 'though I admit that,
by family tradition and even in our ancient evidents, it is explained *lie-boots*,
means, in its primitive sense, rather sandals; and Caius Caesar, the nephew
and successor of Caius Tiberius, received the agnomen of Caligula, *a caligulis,
sive caligis levioribus, quibus adolescentior usus fuerat in exercitu Germanici
patris sui*. And the *caligae* are also proper to the monastic bodies; for we read
in an ancient Glossarium, upon the rule of St. Benedict, in the Abbey of
St. Amand, that *caligae* were tied with latchets.'

'That will apply to the brogues,' said Fergus.

'It will so, my dear Glennaquoich; and the words are express: *Caligae
dictae sunt quia ligantur; nam socci non ligantur, sed tantum intrommituntur*;
that is, *caligae* are denominated from the ligatures wherewith they are bound;
whereas *socci*, which may be analogous to our mules, whilk the English
denominate slippers, are only slipped upon the feet. The words of the charter
are also alternative, *exuere, seu detrahere*; that is, to *undo*, as in the case of
sandals or brogues, and to *pull off*, as we say vernacularly concerning boots.
Yet I would we had more light; but I fear there is little chance of finding
hereabout any erudite author *de re vestiaria*.'

'I should doubt it very much,' said the Chieftain, looking around on the
straggling Highlanders, who were returning loaded with spoils of the slain,

'though the *res vestiaria* itself seems to be in some request at present.' (301–3)
na not; *sae* so; *anent* with regard to; *brogues and trews* Highland shoes and trousers

We need not construe the Latin to enjoy the fun, which lies in the contrast between the solemnly proffered learning (on a battle-field!) and the practicalities of homely wear, 'breeks', 'brogues', and 'trews'. Yet, as Fergus subsequently tells Waverley, 'the man's whole mind is wrapped up in this ceremony', and although there *may* be a little exaggeration in his saying 'I doubt not but the expected pleasure of performing it was a principal motive with him for taking up arms', Mac-Ivor is certainly not wholly wrong. If I have used the word 'suspect' of the baron's involvement with the '45, it is because he so clearly has been led into it by this spirit of what may best be called Antiquarian Romanticism. Neither a politician like Fergus, nor a single-minded romantic fanatic like Flora, the Baron of Bradwardine sees the Rebellion as a glorious way of believing that the present has become the feudal past. As deluded as Flora's devotion, the baron's nostalgic chivalry points symbolically to a weakness in the rebels rather as does Fergus's tincture of self-advancement. No wonder he survives. For he has been a 'rebel' by learned precept, and in his blend of the academic and romantic he represents no danger to the forces of stability.

And Scott, when all is said and done, emerges as committed to those forces himself. His elegy on the passing of the old Highland order comes not from a sitter-on-the-fence who cannot make up his mind about what he really wants, but from the fair-minded man who knows that history cannot stand still, that there can be no change, even for the better, without loss, suffering, and waste. He knows this, though he does not like it; and, conversely, he is not being hypocritical in giving Fergus's death its tragic dignity, though he wishes for no more threats to the rule of law. Was Shakespeare hypocritical, after all, in giving Harry Hotspur his final due of grandeur?

3

'The Heart of Midlothian'

A large proportion, perhaps a majority, of those who admire Scott today, rate *The Heart of Midlothian* as his best novel. I certainly once felt that way myself, and still rank the book among Scott's finest. It has a concentration, for a good half of its length, which he nowhere equals outside one or two short stories, and it impressively brings together three of his main recurring interests: nationality, religion, and the nature of justice. Without doubt it has positive qualities of greatness.

Yet one can come to feel that *Waverley*, though it lacks the rich organization of *The Heart of Midlothian* at its best, is a more completely satisfying achievement overall. Its virtues may be less thickly spread, but be at the same time more generally distributed through the length of the book. And I hope enough was said in my last chapter to show that *Waverley* has real density of texture and foci of interest.

Nevertheless, for density and focus the first half of *The Heart of Midlothian* is unique in Scott's novels. Though I would no longer maintain, as I did in my early days of admiration for the book, that its serious interest ends almost exactly halfway through, with the conclusion of Effie Deans's trial, it still seems to me that its major quality is most convincingly manifest up to that point. Thereafter we find plenty that is central to Scott's preoccupations, but in a relatively dilute form; and though the very late chapters show a clear relevance to those interests, they exhibit a disappointing falling-off in power.

Our first concern, however, must be with what gives *The Heart of Midlothian* its qualities of greatness, and I shall begin by looking at the way in which Scott handles one of the central subjects referred to above: the nature of justice.

Crudely to indicate the novel's approach, it is as though Scott were asking 'What does human justice amount to?' Human justice, we know, has as its monument the institutions of the law, which in this book's context is specifically manifested in the workings of a notorious statute. It is 1736 (not long, we note, after the Union); child-murder has become alarmingly common in Scotland – so common that the government (in London) has had recourse to the harshest of measures: nothing less than inflicting the death penalty on any woman known to be pregnant, who, while not acknowledging her pregnancy, gives birth to a child but cannot subsequently either produce it or prove that it has died a natural death. In the absence of such defences she will be held guilty of the child's murder, even although the fact of its death cannot be established.

The extraordinary severity of the statute could be in itself a fitting text for discourse on the nature of human justice, but Scott's concern goes far deeper than discussion of this particular instance of its workings. Justice and the law, in one form or another, permeate *The Heart of Midlothian* from the start. The opening chapter, in which the imagined teller of the tale falls in with two young men of the law through a rather comical accident, and receives in consequence the substance of 'the following narrative, founded upon the conversation of the evening', is far more than a piece of mechanism designed to set the story in motion. Given Scott's concern with justice, the fact that the two men are lawyers has significance. Of a lively, even somewhat frivolous disposition, they are 'in the heyday of youth and good spirits'; with 'the good sense, taste, and information which their conversation exhibited' is mingled 'An air of giddy gaiety'. The narrator thinks of them as forming 'a very happy mixture of good-breeding and liberal information, with a disposition to lively rattle, pun, and jest, amusing to a grave man, because it is what he himself can least easily command'.

Travelling with them on the overturned coach is a disconsolate creature lately discharged from imprisonment for debt, whose history is known to one of the pair. His colleague remarks that the man 'looks as if he were just about to honour with his residence THE HEART OF MIDLOTHIAN', and there follows this exchange:

'You are mistaken: he is just delivered from it. Our friend here looks for an explanation. Pray, Mr. Pattieson, have you been in Edinburgh?'

I answered in the affirmative.

'Then you must have passed, occasionally at least, though probably not so faithfully as I am doomed to do, through a narrow intricate passage, leading out of the north-west corner of the Parliament Square, and passing by a high and antique building, with turrets and iron grates,

> Making good the saying odd,
> Near the church and far from God' –

Mr. Halkit broke in upon his learned counsel, to contribute his moiety to the riddle – 'Having at the door the sign of the Red Man – '

'And being on the whole,' resumed the counsellor, interrupting his friend in his turn, 'a sort of place where misfortune is happily confounded with guilt, where all who are in wish to get out – '

'And where none who have the good luck to be out wish to get in,' added his companion.

'I conceive you, gentlemen,' replied I: 'you mean the prison.'

'The prison,' added the young lawyer. 'You have hit it – the very reverend tolbooth itself.'   (7–8)

Here, in the deliberately pompous circumlocutions, the conscious verbal virtuosity, the tossing of the riddle from one man to the other, we have the 'giddy gaiety' with a vengeance. And the effect of this oral horse-play, especially when thought of in relation to later developments, is interesting. Is it such men as these, we are inclined to ask, who guide those whose function it is to dispense justice? One does not suppose that the narrator must be seen as mistaken in liking them, and that Scott intends us to think them thoroughly unattractive. On the contrary, their light-heartedness and high spirits come across as agreeable enough in themselves. Only the context in which they are exhibited may tempt us to pass marginal judgement on them as somewhat callous individuals: callous in a manner often associated, not always fairly, with the conversation of young medical students. Later, when we find Effie Deans under threat of death for a murder she has not committed, that epigram about the tolbooth as 'a sort of place where misfortune is happily confounded with guilt', so pathetically applicable to her case, takes on a sadly bitter irony far removed from the frothy gusto with which it is uttered.

The continuation of the passage confirms the impression that the pair are at least as devoted to verbal pyrotechnic as to justice:

'Then the tolbooth of Edinburgh is called the Heart of Midlothian?' said I.

'So termed and reputed, I assure you.'

'I think,' said I, with the bashful diffidence with which a man lets slip a pun in the presence of his superiors, 'the metropolitan county may, in that case, be said to have a sad heart.'

'Right as my glove, Mr. Pattieson,' added Mr. Hardie; 'and a close heart, and a hard heart. Keep it up, Jack.'

'And a wicked heart, and a poor heart,' answered Halkit, doing his best.

'And yet it may be called in some sort a strong heart, and a high heart,' rejoined the advocate. 'You see I can put you both out of heart.'

'I have played all my hearts,' said the younger gentleman.

'Then we'll have another lead,' answered his companion.   (8-9)

The narrator, to be sure, has started the ball rolling, but his venture into wordplay comes from thoughts of the 'sad' plight of prisoners in the tolbooth, whereas the others simply grasp it as a challenge to scintillate. Seen alongside such displays of witty combat, even Hardie's subsequent purple patch of rhetoric about the tolbooth, for all the apparent solemnity of his tone, affects one as springing more from his pleasure in his own fluency than from much in the way of feeling for the human tragedies connected with the place. ('Since that time how many hearts have throbbed within these walls, as the tolling of the neighbouring bell announced to them how fast the sands of their lives were ebbing; how many must have sunk at the sound; how many were supported by stubborn pride and dogged resolution; how many by the consolations of religion?') Mr Pattieson's description of him, during a pause in the exuberant oration, as 'my rattling entertainer', seems exactly right.

But we must recall that the young men have earlier been described as a 'mixture', a word which aptly suggests both our feelings about them and the complexity of response aroused by the best parts of the book. For it is impossible to take a simple view of the pair. While one might be inclined to look sometimes with disapprobation at their verbal antics, there is no guarantee of rightness in the feeling. Hardie's rhetoric, after all, *might* be quite 'serious' at bottom. In neither of them, assuredly, does frolic necessarily point to folly.

The end of Chapter I tellingly underlines this sense of a 'mixture' before the story proper begins. While waiting at the inn after their accident, the lawyers have scented, from the landlord's information, good professional prey in the local political affair of the boroughs of Bubbleburgh and Bitem. 'Like eagles,' we are told, 'they smelled the battle afar off, ordered a magnum of claret and beds at the Wallace, and entered at full career into the Bubbleburgh and Bitem politics, with all the probable "petitions and complaints" to which they were likely to give rise.' Yes, they are very definitely professionals to their fingertips, and one reaction may be that the law is, indeed, *just* a 'profession' to them. That impression could well be strengthened by the sentence which concludes the narrator's encounter with them as he retires to his own home: 'The two young men ordered a broiled bone, Madeira negus, and a pack of cards, and commenced a game at picquet.' Here is one kind of game; we have heard something of their verbal games. Do they perhaps see the law also as a 'game', on maybe a not very different level?

As the chapter's last paragraph begins, we seem to find the suspicion confirmed. What could look more essentially trivial, more a matter of squeezing the utmost advantage out of lucrative muddles, than their subsequent fortunes?

Next morning the travellers left Gandercleugh. I afterwards learned from the papers that both have been since engaged in the great political cause of Bubbleburgh and Bitem, a summary case, and entitled to particular despatch; but which, it is thought, nevertheless, may outlast the duration of the parliament to which the contest refers. (15)

Those words are indeed an ironic comment on the legal exploitation of futility. But very soon our impression of the pair begins to change, as the narrator tells us of the results of the encounter for their unhappy fellow-traveller Dunover, the lately released debtor:

And both the young gentlemen deserve their good fortune; for I learned from Dunover, who called on me some weeks afterwards, and communicated the intelligence with tears in his eyes, that their interest had availed to procure him a small office for the decent maintenance of his family; and that, after a train of constant and uninterrupted misfortune, he could trace a dawn of prosperity to his having the good fortune to be flung from the top of a mail-

coach into the river Gander, in company with an advocate and a writer to the
signet. (15–16)

The effect of all this is interesting and important. Not only are the
two young professionals now seen to be far from callous; there is,
through their behaviour to Dunover, the notion suggested of quite
a different kind of 'justice' from that which they officially serve.
The discussion of *Guy Mannering* (see Chapter 4) will show that
'justice' is a very relative term for Scott, as it must be for anyone
who pauses to consider the various things it can mean. To Scott,
though, goes the credit for deliberately highlighting this variety
of interpretation, and making of it one of a novel's structural
principles. In *The Heart of Midlothian*, where 'justice' in the
strictly legal sense is so much to the fore, this matter of Dunover's good fortune, coming so early in the book, throws everything into ironic perspective. Dunover, it could be said, has
humanly never had 'anything like justice', yet now, after his re-
lease from the prison into which something called 'justice' has cast
him, an apparently unlucky accident has led to a new beginning.

This first chapter, then, should alert the reader to look critically
at the various forms of 'justice' to which appeals are made by this
or that person or group during the ensuing narrative. The story
proper commences, after that obliquely ironic preface, with a
description of the spot that is shortly to witness the most violent
scene in the book, and is to be felt as a presence throughout the
entire drama:

In former times, England had her Tyburn, to which the devoted victims of
justice were conducted in solemn procession up what is now called Oxford
Road. In Edinburgh, a large open street, or rather oblong square, surrounded
by high houses, called the Grass-market, was used for the same melancholy
purpose. It was not ill chosen for such a scene, being of considerable extent,
and therefore fit to accommodate a great number of spectators, such as are
usually assembled by this melancholy spectacle. On the other hand, few of
the houses which surround it were, even in early times, inhabited by persons
of fashion; so that those likely to be offended or over deeply affected by such
unpleasant exhibitions were not in the way of having their quiet disturbed by
them. The houses in the Grassmarket are, generally speaking, of a mean
description; yet the place is not without some features of grandeur, being
overhung by the southern side of the huge rock on which the castle stands,
and by the moss-grown battlements and turreted walls of that ancient fortress.

(17)

The passage has several points of special interest. First there is the irony of that phrase 'the devoted victims of justice'.

The kind of justice which leads to executions, imprisonments, or statutory penalties of any type, is always supposed to be exercised for the good of the society in which it has been instituted. Even oppressively dictatorial régimes, which to outsiders appear to be mocking justice, make a show of having the community's interests at heart. Assuming, therefore, that justice has at least officially worthy purposes behind it (and Scott is not dealing, in *The Heart of Midlothian*, with governmental tyranny in any ordinary sense), the fact that it should be spoken of as having 'victims' cannot but jar. We know quite well, of course, what Scott means: to call these people 'victims' is a way of saying that they have broken the established law and are punished accordingly. But the word has overtones which continue to sound in the mind. Here the dictionary is useful, for although reliance upon the dictionary definition can be most misleading where imaginative writing is concerned, one finds in this case some explanation of the word's uncomfortable reverberations: 'Victim. 1497. . . . 1. A living creature killed and offered as a sacrifice to some deity or supernatural power. 2. A person who is put to death or subjected to torture by another; one who suffers severely in body or property through cruel or oppressive treatment 1660. b. One who is reduced or destined to suffer under some oppressive or destructive agency 1718. c. One who perishes or suffers in health, etc. from some exercise or pursuit voluntarily undertaken 1726. d. In weaker sense: One who suffers some injury, hardship, or loss, is badly treated or taken advantage of, or the like 1781.' (*The Shorter Oxford English Dictionary*, third edition.) Only 'c', if one thinks about it, carries a suggestion that the fate of a 'victim' of *justice* would in a sense be self-inflicted and deserved, for a punishable crime usually results from a 'pursuit voluntarily undertaken'. The remaining definitions under '2' all have associations of cruelty and oppression. And even '1', though less immediately apt to the context acquires an additionally disturbing relevance when thought of in the light of the qualifying adjective 'devoted': '1. Vowed; dedicated, consecrated. 2. Characterized by devotion

1600. 3. Doomed 1611.' (*S.O.E.D.*) Of those definitions '2' gives the word its most familiar modern sense, which clearly, like 'vowed' or 'dedicated', will not do. 'Doomed', however, is utterly in keeping (later the great trial scene introduces a weird functionary called the Doomster), and although the idea of a condemned man as 'doomed to die' is ordinary in itself, when it is taken in conjunction with 'consecrated' and with the notion of sacrifice in the first definition of 'victim' it implies a sense of 'justice' as some kind of extra-human force or deity – existing, it would outwardly appear, for the sake of humans, yet in reality coldly pursuing its own non-human (or inhuman) ends. Scott is no anarchist or advocate of legal iconoclasm, but *The Heart of Midlothian* does make one reflect on the tendency of legal institutions to become self-perpetuating monuments of their own magnificence.

A second point of interest concerns what most readers would be initially disposed to reckon a stylistic fault: the seemingly clumsy use of 'melancholy' in the same place at the end of two adjacent sentences, and a similarly infelicitous grouping of 'spectators' and 'spectacle' in the second of them: 'In Edinburgh, a large open street, or rather oblong square, surrounded by high houses, called the Grass-market, was used for the same *melancholy purpose*. It was not ill chosen for such a scene, being of considerable extent, and therefore fit to accommodate a great number of *spectators*, such as are usually assembled by this *melancholy spectacle*.' One must guard against special pleading, since Scott can be, and more often than not is, quite genuinely clumsy in his weaker novels. But here the apparently infelicitous turns out to have felicity. In this connection it is useful to continue on to the first sentence of the next paragraph: 'It was the custom, until within these thirty years or thereabouts, to use this esplanade for the scene of public executions.' Most of us will not have witnessed such an event, while being aware that the public execution, as a deterrent exhibition before a mass audience, is by no means unknown to the modern world. Nor, one gathers, are the occasions on which it is practised notably under-attended. And that prompts a remark on a third point arising out of the passage: one should not look on the events of 1736 in Edinburgh with a cosy sense of their remoteness, geographical or chronological. Scott's probing of the workings of justice has both permanent and universal significance. To return to the second point (the working of the apparent stylistic clumsiness), what the repetition of 'melancholy' does is point to the sheer brutal perversity of those who assembled to watch other people being killed. In the phrase 'melancholy *purpose*' we have merely a sad acceptance of the fact that executions, if the law provides for them, have to be carried out somewhere, sometimes, however much we may regret it. In 'melancholy *spectacle*', on the other hand, what ought to be thought of as depressing though necessary has become an occasion for public entertainment, the point being pressed home by the close proximity of 'spectators'. One has the rather horrible feeling of the crowds as being composed of sadistic *voyeurs*, perversely fascinated by both the fact and the apparatus of legal killing.

There follows a compact account of the arrest of two criminals, Wilson and Robertson, the escape of Robertson, the execution of his accomplice, and the ensuing public tumult, as a result of which Captain Porteous, Commander of the City Guard, is tried and sentenced to death for wrongfully opening fire on innocent people. The day appointed for his execution in the Grassmarket arrives, only to bring to the great mob gathered for the sight the news that he has been reprieved:

The assembled spectators of almost all degrees, whose minds had been wound up to the pitch which we have described, uttered a groan, or rather a roar of indignation and disappointed revenge, similar to that of a tiger from whom his meal has been rent by his keeper when he was just about to devour it. (35)

The 'justice' of the mob, as manifested there, is brutal and radically inhuman; yet, paradoxically, in a way, more motivated by human *feeling* than the official justice of the law. The law, by exercise of reason, finds extenuating factors in the crime of Porteous. The mob, on the other hand, swayed only by passion, by an instinctive sense of moral outrage, demands 'Blood for blood'. Now in this instance, unsympathetic though Porteous is, we side with the reason of the law rather than with the passion, aroused by unthinking and unbalancing instincts, of the mob. But later on that same reasoned, calculating legal justice will appear in its turn inhuman. The question is, which kind of 'justice' do we consider, in the end, to be the more 'just'?

As the disappointed crowd disperses, we have our first sight of the boldly drawn vernacular gossips, who function rather as choric commentators on the action. The macabre humour of their very first exchange contains references to the law:

> 'An unco thing this, Mrs. Howden,' said old Peter Plumdamas to his neighbour the rouping-wife, or saleswoman, as he offered her his arm to assist her in the toilsome ascent, 'to see the grit folk at Lunnon set their face against law and gospel, and let loose sic a reprobate as Porteous upon a peaceable town!'
> 'And to think o' the weary walk they hae gien us,' answered Mrs. Howden, with a groan; 'and sic a comfortable window as I had gotten, too, just within a pennystane cast of the scaffold – I could hae heard every word the minister said – and to pay twal pennies for my stand, and a' for naething!' (37)
> *unco* uncommon, extraordinary; *grit* great; *sic* such; *hae gien* have given; *within a pennystane cast* within a stone's throw; *twal* twelve; *a' for naething* all for nothing

The ridiculous Bartoline Saddletree, who fancies himself as a legal authority, has the effect, in his overwhelming outpourings of legal jargon, of making the law sound like an arid and absurd mechanism of phrases and abstractions, quite unconnected with the human beings it is supposed to govern:

> Saddletree was laying down, with great precision, the law upon Porteous's case, by which he arrived at this conclusion, that, if Porteous had fired five minutes sooner, before Wilson was cut down, he would have been *versans in licito*, engaged, that is, in a lawful act, and only liable to be punished *propter excessum* or for lack of discretion, which might have mitigated the punishment to *poena ordinaria*. (38)

It is typical of the unobtrusive smoothness of Scott's art in the best parts of this novel that he should introduce the central issue, the case of Effie Deans, almost casually, as an incidental in the talk of the gossips:

> 'Come, come, Mr. Saddletree,' said his wife, 'we'll hae nae confessions and condescendences here, let them deal in thae sort o' wares that are paid for them; they suit the like o' us as ill as a demi-pique saddle would suit a draught ox.'
> 'Aha!' said Mr. Butler, '*Optat ephippia bos piger*, nothing new under the sun. But it was a fair hit of Mrs. Saddletree, however.'

'And it wad far better become ye, Mr. Saddletree,' continued his helpmate, 'since ye say ye hae skeel o' the law, to try if ye can do ony thing for Effie Deans, puir thing, that's lying up in the tolbooth yonder, cauld, and hungry, and comfortless.' (45)

skeel skill; *puir* poor; *cauld* cold

And the first we hear of the statute under which Effie is to be tried is from the lips of the absurd Saddletree:

'The case of Effie – or Euphemia – Deans,' resumed Saddletree, 'is one of those cases of murder presumptive, that is, a murder of the law's inferring or construction, being derived from certain *indicia* or grounds of suspicion.'

'So that,' said the good woman, 'unless puir Effie has communicated her situation, she'll be hanged by the neck, if the bairn was still-born, or if it be alive at this moment?'

'Assuredly,' said Saddletree, 'it being a statute made by our sovereign Lord and Lady to prevent the horrid delict of bringing forth children in secret. The crime is rather a favourite of the law, this species of murther being one of its ain creation.'

'Then, if the law makes murders,' said Mrs. Saddletree, 'the law should be hanged for them; or if they wad hang a lawyer instead, the country wad find nae faut.'

A summons to their frugal dinner interrupted the further progress of the conversation, which was otherwise like to take a turn much less favourable to the science of jurisprudence and its professors than Mr. Bartoline Saddletree, the fond admirer of both, had at its opening anticipated. (48–9)

bairn child; *ain* own; *wad find nae faut* would find no fault

Saddletree in himself is not to be taken seriously, but the extreme and cold-blooded vision he gives of the law's workings plays its part in the total ironic probing of the nature of justice. The reaction of his wife to the details of the statute, on the other hand, is that of the ordinary good-hearted person, to whom the apparatus of legal institutions seems inhuman as well as bewildering.

It is that same human instinctive view of justice, however, which inspires the mob who, in Chapters 6 and 7, seize control of the tolbooth, drag out the reprieved Porteous, and brutally hang him, forcing Reuben Butler (the somewhat insipid clergyman who later marries Jeanie Deans) to be present and officiating. Horrified at what is afoot, Butler imperils his own life by trying to reason with the rioters in the name of both secular and divine justice, but the only response he receives is the 'Blood must have blood' of their crudely simplifying, though perfectly understandable, desire to avenge the lives of the persons whose death Porteous caused:

Butler, who, in great terror and anxiety, had been detained within a few yards of the tolbooth door, to wait the event of the search after Porteous, was now brought forward and commanded to walk by the prisoner's side, and to prepare him for immediate death. His answer was a supplication that the rioters would consider what they did. 'You are neither judges nor jury,' said he. 'You cannot have, by the laws of God or man, power to take away the life of a human creature, however deserving he may be of death. If it is murder even in a lawful magistrate to execute an offender otherwise than in the place, time, and manner which the judge's sentence prescribes, what must it be in you, who have no warrant for interference but your own wills? In the name of Him who is all mercy, show mercy to this unhappy man, and do not dip your hands in his blood, nor rush into the very crime which you are desirous of avenging!'

'Cut your sermon short, you are not in your pulpit,' answered one of the rioters.

'If we hear more of your clavers,' said another, 'we are like to hang you up beside him.'

'Peace! hush!' said Wildfire. 'Do the good man no harm; he discharges his conscience, and I like him the better.'

He then addressed Butler. 'Now, sir, we have patiently heard you, and we just wish you to understand, in the way of answer, that you may as well argue to the ashler-work and iron stanchels of the tolbooth as think to change our purpose. Blood must have blood. We have sworn to each other by the deepest oaths ever were pledged, that Porteous shall die the death he deserves so richly.' (64)

clavers silly talk

We are swiftly introduced, after that grim episode, to the fierce old Nonconformist David Deans, whose daughter lies in prison on the charge of infanticide. The old man is overcome by Effie's disgrace and the probability of her eventual execution, but, fanatical in his narrow religious enthusiasm, he declares 'if a dollar, or a plack, or the nineteenth part of a boddle wad save her open guilt and open shame frae open punishment, that purchase wad David Deans never make. Na, na; an eye for an eye, a tooth for a tooth, life for life, blood for blood: it's the law of man, and it's the law of God.' Divine justice, in the old man's view, is no more tempered with reason or mercy than the justice of the mob, and the likely punishment awaiting Effie here seems to him – though he wavers later in the book – a completely just divine retribution.

55

In a meeting with Robertson, Effie's seducer, the sister of the unfortunate girl learns that Effie is certainly innocent of the death of her child, but that she can be saved only if Jeanie will perjure herself at the trial, by making the false statement that her sister had told her of her condition, thus clearing her of the charge of concealing her pregnancy. This Jeanie cannot bring herself to agree to. Robertson regards the law as an inhuman mechanism which in this case can easily be circumvented by a simple falsehood. But to Jeanie more than the law is involved:

'I wad ware the best blood in my body to keep her skaithless,' said Jeanie, weeping in bitter agony; 'but I canna change right into wrang, or make that true which is false.'

'Foolish, hard-hearted girl,' said the stranger, 'are you afraid of what they may do to you? I tell you, even the retainers of the law, who course life as greyhounds do hares, will rejoice at the escape of a creature so young—so beautiful; that they will not suspect your tale; that, if they did suspect it, they would consider you as deserving, not only of forgiveness, but of praise for your natural affection.'

'It is not man I fear,' said Jeanie, looking upward; 'the God, whose name I must call on to witness the truth of what I say, He will know the falsehood.'

'And He will know the motive,' said the stranger, eagerly; 'He will know that you are doing this, not for lucre of gain, but to save the life of the innocent, and prevent the commission of a worse crime than that which the law seeks to avenge.'

'He has given us a law,' said Jeanie, 'for the lamp of our path; if we stray from it we err against knowledge. I may not do evil, even that good may come out of it.'   (158–9)

ware expend; *skaithless* out of harm; *canna* cannot; *wrang* wrong

When the day of the trial arrives, Jeanie, sworn in truthfulness to a law she honours above the law of man, whether it is motivated by instinct or by reason, cannot bring herself to utter the required falsehood, in spite of Effie's agonized cry, 'Oh, Jeanie, Jeanie, save me, save me!' and the hearing ends with the passing of the death sentence.

Fair though the conduct of the trial is, this same legal justice which has taken so much the more desirable of the two views of the Porteous affair, here seems coldly inhuman in its efficiency. The description of the court-house suggests, like the talk of the young lawyers in Chapter I (before we are made to reconsider them), calm indifference and chilling professionalism on the part of the law towards the human beings it is its function to serve:

> Admitted within the precincts of the court-house, they found the usual number of busy office-bearers and idle loiterers, who attend on these scenes by choice or from duty. Burghers gaped and stared; young lawyers sauntered, sneered, and laughed, as in the pit of the theatre; while others apart sat on a bench retired and reasoned highly, *inter apices juris*, on the doctrines of constructive crime and the true import of the statute. (220)

And with the ritual appearance, at the conclusion of the trial, of the Doomster, 'a tall haggard figure, arrayed in a fantastic garment of black and gray, passmented with silver lace', from whom 'all fell back with a sort of instinctive horror', comes a note almost of barbarism. What, we feel inclined to ask, is such a figure doing in the legal institutions of a supposedly civilized society?

Effie Deans does not, of course, die, and there remains plenty to interest one in the rest of the novel: Jeanie's adventures in travelling to London to seek her sister's reprieve, the meeting with Queen Caroline, the facts about Robertson, and the subsequent fortunes of the two sisters. But the book's most concentrated art, the art which makes us think 'all round' the subject of justice, culminates with Effie's words at the end of the trial, together with the ensuing paragraph. What Effie says may be taken as the traditional Christian comment on the question 'What does human justice amount to?':

> 'God forgive ye, my lords,' she said, 'and dinna be angry wi' me for wishing it – we a' need forgiveness. As for myself, I canna blame ye, for ye act up to your lights; and if I havena killed my poor infant, ye may witness a' that hae seen it this day, that I hae been the means of killing my grey-headed father. I deserve the warst frae man, and frae God too. But God is mair mercifu' to us than we are to each other.' (248)
>
> *dinna* do not; *warst* worst; *mair* more

And immediately afterwards, as though in illustration of her words, we have this picture of the indifference of both mob and law. The two extremes of human justice are brought to one level:

> With these words the trial concluded. The crowd rushed, bearing forward and shouldering each other, out of the court in the same tumultuary mode in which they had entered; and, in the excitation of animal motion and animal spirits, soon forgot whatever they had felt as impressive in the scene which

57

they had witnessed. The professional spectators, whom habit and theory had rendered as callous to the distress of the scene as medical men are to those of a surgical operation, walked homeward in groups, discussing the general principle of the statute under which the young woman was condemned, the nature of the evidence, and the arguments of the counsel, without considering even that of the Judge as exempt from their criticism. (248)

It would be wrong to suppose, however, that this is Scott's last word on the subject of justice in *The Heart of Midlothian*. Clearly Jeanie's appeal to Queen Caroline, though the interview has other important ramifications, carries on his exploration of the theme, bringing together, in Jeanie's simple though forceful presentation of her case, instinctive 'human' justice, respect for the law of the land, and a sense of what is 'just' according to her religious tenets. With the reappearance, late in the novel, of Effie Deans as Lady Staunton, and of her seducer 'Robertson' as Sir George Staunton, we move to a treatment of 'justice' on a different level: as destiny, receiving one's deserts for past conduct through mental unease or the workings of aptly retributory forces, as 'poetic justice'. Sir George dies in a fight involving his unrecognized son (a bestial ruffian known simply as 'the Whistler'), and there is good reason to believe that the long-sought boy has himself been the killer. As for his widow, Scott has this to say about her later years:

After blazing nearly ten years in the fashionable world, and hiding, like many of her compeers, an aching heart with a gay demeanour, after declining repeated offers of the most respectable kind for a second matrimonial engagement, Lady Staunton betrayed the inward wound by retiring to the Continent and taking up her abode in the convent where she had received her education. She never took the veil, but lived and died in severe seclusion, and in the practice of the Roman Catholic religion, in all its formal observances, vigils, and austerities. (537)

We are plainly meant to see the 'inward wound' not only as grief at her husband's death, but also as the working of a conscience unquiet since the days of her early involvement with him:

READER – This tale will not be told in vain, if it shall be found to illustrate the great truth that guilt, though it may attain temporal splendour, can never confer real happiness; that the evil consequences of our crimes long survive their commission, and, like the ghosts of the murdered, for ever haunt the steps of the malefactor; and that the paths of virtue, though seldom those of worldly greatness, are always those of pleasantness and peace.   (538)

With that sternly moralistic utterance *The Heart of Midlothian* ends – apart from a facetious postscript which makes one feel that Scott was uneasy at such austere finger-wagging. And indeed it is remarkably out of key with the best things in the novel, suggesting a rigidity of attitude quite remote from their flexibility and fairness. It accounts, though, for the relative inferiority of the book's later chapters; for while the concern with 'poetic justice' does add a dimension to Scott's design, one has the feeling that Jeanie and Reuben Butler are all too charmingly rewarded for their virtue (the few little vicissitudes only point this up) and the Stauntons all too relentlessly hounded for the reverse. From being a subtle novel which enlarges one's sympathies, one's sense of what it is to be human, *The Heart of Midlothian* has become a comparatively crude moralistic tale. 'Poetic justice' is more effectively handled in *Guy Mannering*.

Without pressing the idea too far, one might suggest that the parting address to the READER sounds not unlike David Deans in characteristic hellfire vein. This is very odd, considering that Scott was no David Deans himself, and even odder when we think of the ways in which he actually handles the doughty old Puritan. Not that he treats him as a ridiculous figure, as a mere caricature. Much of what is best in the book would be lost if this were so. But Scott nevertheless extracts a deal of comedy from the old man's extreme religious enthusiasm. It would be out of place in a study like the present one to rehearse the historical background to David's religious position. Suffice it to say that he looks back with regret to what he sees as the great and glorious days of Scottish dissent, before the national church was 'infected' by the spirit of backsliding accommodation which he associates with England and the Union. His attitude to the Scottish church of 1736 is rather like that of a doctrinaire orthodox Communist towards 're-visionists'.

But although we are often made to smile at the old man's tub-thumping reminiscences of the faithful, we cannot regard him as a 'simple' character. If, as I have tried to show, the Baron of

Bradwardine in *Waverley* is less straightforward than outwardly appears, David Deans arouses more complex responses still. He has his tirades, to be sure, as the baron has his erudite outpourings, but they engage our attention and stimulate our judgement in a way that the baron's sometimes overworked verbiage does not. Take the following, from Chapter 10, which puts in context a passage quoted earlier in this discussion. David is coming to himself after the first shock of horror at Effie's disgrace. The fatuous Laird of Dumbiedikes characteristically pulls out his purse, supposing that money will somehow help the situation:

The old man had now raised himself from the ground, and, looking about him as if he missed something, seemed gradually to recover the sense of his wretchedness. 'Where,' he said, with a voice that made the roof ring – 'where is the vile harlot that has disgraced the blood of an honest man? Where is she that has no place among us, but has come foul with her sins, like the Evil One, among the children of God? Where is she, Jeanie? Bring her before me, that I may kill her with a word and a look!'

All hastened around him with their appropriate sources of consolation – the Laird with his purse, Jeanie with burnt feathers and strong waters, and the women with their exhortations. 'O neighbour – O Mr. Deans, it's a sair trial, doubtless; but think of the Rock of Ages, neighbour, think of the promise!'

'And I do think of it, neighbours, and I bless God that I can think of it, even in the wrack and ruin of a' that's nearest and dearest to me. But to be the father of a castaway, a profligate, a bloody Zipporah, a mere murderess! O, how will the wicked exult in the high places of their wickedness! – the prelatists, and the latitudinarians, and the hand-waled murderers, whose hands are hard as horn wi' hauding the slaughter-weapons; they will push out the lip, and say that we are even such as themselves. Sair, sair I am grieved, neighbours, for the poor castaway, for the child of mine old age; but sairer for the stumbling-block and scandal it will be to all tender and honest souls!'

'Davie, winna siller do't?' insinuated the Laird, still proffering his green purse, which was full of guineas.

'I tell ye, Dumbiedikes,' said Deans, 'that if telling down my haill substance could hae saved her frae this black snare, I wad hae walked out wi' naething but my bonnet and my staff to beg an awmous for God's sake, and ca'd mysell an happy man. But if a dollar, or a plack, or the nineteenth part of a boddle wad save her open guilt and open shame frae open punishment, that purchase wad David Deans never make. Na, na; an eye for an eye, a tooth for a tooth, life for life, blood for blood: it's the law of man, and it's the law of God. Leave me, sirs – leave me; I maun warstle wi' this trial in privacy and on my knees.'

Jeanie, now in some degree restored to the power of thought, joined in the same request. The next day found the father and daughter still in the depth of affliction, but the father sternly supporting his load of ill through a proud sense of religious duty, and the daughter anxiously suppressing her own feelings to avoid awakening his. (105–6)

sair sore; *hand-waled* hand-picked; *wi' hauding* with holding; *winna siller do't* won't money do it; *a dollar or a plack, or the nineteenth part of a boddle* references to very small coins; *haill* whole; *maun warstle* must wrestle

How, exactly, do we react to all that? The passage certainly offers a very odd mixture, for although the situation it concerns is anything but funny, the comic is obviously there. We have it not only in David's rant about 'the prelatists, and the latitudinarians, and the hand-waled murderers' (one need not know the precise references to see the funny side of this, any more than one has to follow the baron's Latin), but also in the pious 'exhortations' of the women, and of course in the nonsensical laird. At the same time, we cannot but feel genuine pity for the old man (not to mention pity for Jeanie), 'in the wrack and ruin' of Effie's disaster. Yet this in turn is qualified by some doubt as to what 'a' that's nearest and dearest' to David really *is*. One naturally supposes that it must be his unfortunate daughter, but the ending of that part of his outburst brings in the suspicion that the phrase may more properly refer to 'all tender and honest souls': like-minded co-religionists, that is to say. And that impression is of course strengthened by his echoing of the 'justice' at whose dictates Porteous dies. Neither reason, nor feeling for blood-ties, it would seem, can sway him, only this savagely stern belief in a mercilessly avenging deity. Well may our pity for the old father find itself turning into impatience, or even disgust. But once more reflection makes us reconsider. Does David Deans not protest too much? Does his 'proud sense of religious duty' *really* mean more to him than Effie's fate? Are his outbursts not probably a means of trying, in the face of the blow, to stay sane? Moreover, as the rest of the novel shows, he is not always so extreme in his sectarianism. Much later on, for example, we find him anxious, even alarmed, lest the rigour of his arguments (for it is a vein that is second nature to him) should have made Reuben Butler decide against accepting the living of Knocktarlitie; and despite his abhorrence of the Union, he manages to have a good word for Queen Caroline. For all the mixed feelings that he arouses, including the amusement, David

Deans has a genuine representative impressiveness, for in him we see embodied a whole page of the religious history of Scotland. His alternations of thundering Biblical rhetoric and inescapable personal emotion (we can glimpse the onset of the latter when he leaves to 'warstle wi' this trial in privacy') symbolically reflect the conflict between what remained of the old-style strict Presbyterian of the seventeenth century and the social and political changes which were inevitably affecting the spirit of the Scottish church. Here again Scott is the historical novelist in the best sense.

Through David Deans, then, this novel's preoccupations with religion, justice, and nationality, are brought together. But this is done in other ways as well, particularly with regard to nationality. Those readers who do not know Scotland or any Scottish people may find it a little hard to realize just how strong the feeling of nationhood has been and still is in that northern part of Britain. To understand this must be especially difficult in former British colonies, where the visible local manifestation of Britain was so often a Scotsman. Yet although it would be factually incorrect, at the moment, to say that the majority of Scots desire a return to pre-Union independence, there is no doubt that the Scot thinks of himself as 'Scottish' first and 'British' second. University applications, for example, from Scottish candidates, more often than not state the nationality to be 'Scottish', though from an international point of view their nationality is simply 'British'. And in *The Heart of Midlothian* we find this ambiguity writ large, running parallel to the religious ambiguity symbolically expressed by the conflict in David Deans.

When we remember that the action of the novel is set not quite thirty years after the Union, we can see just why the Porteous affair figures so centrally. While knowing that in *theory* they are British, the Edinburgh people who are so incensed by the reprieve of Porteous see the last-minute move as a contemptuous blow to Scottish opinion. True, the parliament in London is supposed to be as much a Scottish parliament as an English one, but the loss of the old specifically Scottish government, there on the spot, in Edinburgh, strikes them as a step towards domination by indifferent aliens in a far-off city. To Queen Caroline, on the other hand, the killing of Porteous is seen as a barbarous challenge to her authority, for she is as much queen of Scotland as she is queen of England, and her government is supposed to be that of one nation – Britain.

Without imagining that Scott, had he been among the people of Edinburgh in 1736, would have been a party to the hanging of Porteous, one can still feel that he has divided sympathies with regard to the affair. In spite of obvious revulsion at the rioters' cruelty, he gives them their due for courteous treatment of innocents who chanced to be in the vicinity. Moreover, the aggrieved reactions of the people to Porteous's reprieve are given a good hearing. One cannot wholly dismiss, reason notwithstanding, old Peter Plumdamas's complaint that it is a strange and serious thing 'to see the grit folk at Lunnon set their face against law and gospel, and let loose sic a reprobate as Porteous upon a peaceable town!'

Once more we are brought back to the question of Scott's complex make-up. The fiercely patriotic Scotsman *does* feel enraged at slights to his native land, yet the equally patriotic British subject, upholder of Crown and government, has to find a way of reconciling his sense of *local* 'nationality' with his belief in post-Union Britain. In other words, just as his treatment of justice shows him trying to suggest a middle course between purely emotional and purely reasoning justice, so *The Heart of Midlothian* imaginatively tries to work out a way in which he can come to terms with the problem of being loyally British while remaining unrepentantly Scots.

Here the place of Queen Caroline and the Duke of Argyle in the scheme of the book becomes plain. They are certainly not present merely for historical 'colour', but play an essential part in the imaginative debate on nationality. The duke can be taken as representing a position very like the author's. He too is loyal to Crown and government, yet his plain-spoken Scottishness has made him less than popular at Court. Nevertheless, the queen is too astute, too much of a 'politician', to undervalue him, and despite the bitter anger which the killing of Porteous has aroused in her, she will hear, and indeed digest, what the duke has to say. And here again we have symbolism. For the relationship, calculated and calculating, between Caroline and this powerful noble, embodies England's coming to terms with Scotland as a vital part of the kingdom, not as a mere inferior province. And by the same token, the duke's role signifies Scotland's acceptance of this position, provided that she is not deprived of everything traditional in her systems and beliefs: in a word, on condition that Scotland is not de-natured into being no longer Scottish.

Jeanie puts her plea before the queen at what would seem to be the worst possible time. How can one expect a proud ruler, still smarting at Edinburgh's affront, to countenance an ordinary Scots girl's appeal that the provisions of a statute expressly directed at Scotland be relaxed in favour of her sister? As one would expect, the queen at first insists on what is reasonable in the statute, while admitting its deadly severity. But there turns out to be a paradoxical opportuneness in the appearance before her of Jeanie and the Duke of Argyle. The Porteous affair makes it especially desirable that she and her government should have the support of so powerful a Scotsman, and although she is clearly genuinely moved emotionally by the force with which Jeanie puts her plea, her undertaking to see that Effie's reprieve is granted enables her to please the duke without its being openly apparent that she is granting him a *personal* favour. Calculating political reason, *and* sympathetic human emotion, have thus acted, in this situation, to save an innocent girl's life, to produce what might be seen as true justice.

Most modern discussions of *The Heart of Midlothian* put more explicit stress on the role of Jeanie than I have done. Although I would by no means slight her, it seems to me that her significance is a less complex matter than the aspects of the novel I have considered. She has, of course, her conflicts of conscience, which, like the perplexities of her father, are impressively rendered. But it is of the essence of her strength that she should be 'simple': not in a sense suggestive of anything approaching stupidity, rather in that she is unchanging and unswerving amidst so much that is in doubt. For *The Heart of Midlothian* gives us the totally unlooked-for in abundance. Not only is it hard to know what true justice is; it is equally impossible to know what exactly a person *is* or will

64

become. Robertson emerges as Staunton; Effie reappears as a society belle; their child assumes the wild shape of 'the Whistler'; and Madge Wildfire's songs and ramblings are at one moment utterly insane, at another sharply penetrating.

The Heart of Midlothian, then, offers very much of a mixture. At its best it is a great novel; at its second best the book gives us interesting narrative, not without relevance to its great features; at its worst it lets us down with a moralizing bias most unexpected in juxtaposition with the subtlety of so much else; and in one place, unfortunately, though in only one, it tempts us to share the view of those who stress Scott's enslavement by the market. If Fergus Mac-Ivor is a very subtle variant of the Romantic 'hero-villain', 'Robertson', as first seen by Butler, is the perfect stereotype:

> The fiery eye, the abrupt demeanour, the occasionally harsh, yet studiously subdued, tone of voice; the features, handsome, but now clouded with pride, now disturbed by suspicion, now inflamed with passion; those dark hazel eyes which he sometimes shaded with his cap, as if he were averse to have them seen while they were occupied with keenly observing the motions and bearing of others – those eyes that were now turbid with melancholy, now gleaming with scorn, and now sparkling with fury – was it the passions of a mere mortal they expressed, or the emotions of a fiend, who seeks, and seeks in vain, to conceal his fiendish designs under the borrowed mask of manly beauty? The whole partook of the mien, language, and port of the ruined archangel. (112–13)

One may set that beside the description of Conrad, in Byron's The Corsair:

> Though smooth his voice, and calm his general mien,
> Still seems there something he would not have seen;
> His features' deepening lines and varying hue
> At times attracted, yet perplex'd the view,
> As if within that murkiness of mind
> Work'd feelings fearful, and yet undefined;
> Such might it be – that none could truly tell –
> Too close inquiry his stern glance would quell. (Canto the First)

It is not for things like that, pieces of the vaguest sensationalism, that one reads Byron today. The Scott passage, likewise, cannot but jar when surrounded, as it is here in the superior first half of the novel, by so much that is so different.

Let me end this chapter, however, on a positive note. In its disturbing analysis of the nature of justice *The Heart of Midlothian* has a meaning for everyone at all times and in all places; and in its sympathetic awareness of the conflicts and upheavals attendant upon the growth of a new composite state (particularly the dilemma of national dignity versus national advantage), it has a peculiar relevance in the modern world of changing maps and new nations.

4

A Study in Mixtures:
'Guy Mannering'; 'Redgauntlet'; 'The Antiquary'

'Of his books *The Heart of Midlothian* comes the nearest to being a great novel, but hardly *is* that: too many allowances and deductions have to be made.' The force of F. R. Leavis's observation should now be fairly plain. If the word 'mixture' points to much that is most stimulating in *Waverley*, it clearly has a different application to the later novel, whose inconsistencies make one think of it as 'a book with great qualities' rather than, simply, 'a great book'. Great qualities, however, are not to be ignored, whatever the company one finds them in; nor is the civilized intelligence which permits a flexible play of mind (and feeling) over an agglomeration of materials that can seem, when merely catalogued, to be quite extraordinarily heterogeneous. *Waverley*, of course, like all Scott's best work, clearly shows the functioning of such an intelligence, but despite that novel's complexities it does not range over so odd a farrago of assorted matter as the three books which are the subject of this chapter.

Here it is useful to look at another part of F. R. Leavis's footnote (for the whole quotation see Chapter I): '(Scott) was a great and very intelligent man; but, not having the creative writer's interest in literature, he made no serious attempt to work out his own form and break away from the bad tradition of the eighteenth-century romance.' One might query that assertion of the absence, in Scott, of 'the creative writer's interest in literature': was he, then, *just* a commercial author? Are we to take his disparaging remarks, to friends and others, on the business of writing, with absolute seriousness? When he achieves greatness, or something close to greatness, is it purely by accident?

My own answer to those questions is that I would not be writing this book if I had to come out with a barely qualified 'Yes'. But in a more important sense than the questions suggest, Leavis has much right on his side. Scott was often anxious as to whether or not a novel was 'working out' in a way that would interest his readers; he had his worries about the appeal of his subject-matter; he sometimes had qualms about possible complaints on moral grounds (the ending of *The Heart of Midlothian* fairly obviously shows him trying to guard against them); he had difficulty in bringing some of his plots to a close. With that kind of consideration, however, his expressed awareness of the creative writer's problems more or less begins and ends. We find in Scott no explicit evidence of the care that Dickens took in structuring his novels to be both serious works of literature and stories conforming to the exigencies of serial publication. And if the awareness of being an artist that one meets with in Henry James's notebooks is such as one looks for from very few writers indeed, Scott seems to live in a literary world far removed not only from him, but also from the D. H. Lawrence whose determination to 'get things right' made him work so hard on a book like *Women in Love*. 'Getting things right', and 'working out', would seem for Scott to have been a matter of sustaining 'interest' in plot and providing 'acceptability' in character.

At this point a familiar type of objection must be anticipated: Of what importance is it that Scott overtly expressed no deeper level of concern with being a creative artist? Shakespeare, after all, left no documentary record of the deliberations which produced his plays. Is it not reasonable to suppose that Shakespeare was primarily concerned to make money, and that if he happened to be a great as well as a commercially successful dramatist it was a lucky accident? If Shakespeare, why not Scott? Is not the fact that Scott *could* produce great work, even though without Dickensian or Jamesian or Lawrencian effort, evidence of his possessing the only kind of 'interest in literature' that counts?

In a way such arguments are unanswerable, though saying so means taking them at a level more intelligent than the one at which they are usually advanced. Scott's exploration of the nature of justice in *The Heart of Midlothian* does indeed testify to 'the creative writer's interest in literature'. No one could have carried it out with such flexible vividness who was not intensely aware of what literature, rather than history or legal philosophy, can *do*. And that awareness implies no idea of the literary artist as a pursuer of 'form' for its own sake. If *The Heart of Midlothian*, Robertson's Byronic apparition excluded, impresses us in its first half as a finely shaped whole, it is because the spirit in which Scott examines the complexities of the justice theme has made it like that. The coherence results from the inclusive grip of his imaginative intelligence. Similarly, we need no author's notebook or diary, but only the magnificent development through the plays themselves, to tell us that Shakespeare had 'the creative writer's interest in literature'.

Yet in spite of those reflections, which may seem to justify the arguments under discussion, one must finally reject their terms. One must do this because they basically assume that the great artist is an inspired muddler who gets his results without really knowing or caring, provided that they sell. To that one can only say, with all emphasis, that a distinguished writer's concern to earn his living in no way necessarily precludes awareness of his creative problems at a serious level. Henry James, very overtly aware, was no fool when it came to financial relations with publishers.

What, then, shall we say about the sense in which the Leavis footnote is right? Although no comparison on anything like equal terms between Scott and Shakespeare is being suggested, a brief juxtaposition of the two can help us. Shakespeare, let us say, is the *type* of the artist who moves forward from the literary commonplaces of his time to find his own unique way of speaking. Dickens is another; so is Blake. The distance Shakespeare travels between, for example, *The Two Gentlemen of Verona* and *The Winter's Tale*, shows him working out 'his own form', the working out being at one with a deepening sense of what in human life is to him important. Scott is not that *type* of artist. I think that in the first half of *The Heart of Midlothian* he does work out his own form, and that other novels of his give evidence of similar power. But it is sporadic. The conventions of the ordinary tale of adventure and romance come all too easily to hand. Only when in the grip of matters which profoundly engage his interest does he escape them. Because such matters are practically the whole stuff of *Waverley*, it is Scott's most consistently satisfactory work. If the straightforwardly chronicle narrative seems ordinary enough as a way of telling a story, there is real originality in the shifting perspectives of attitude and the symbolic use of setting. In *The Heart of Midlothian* at its best, on the other hand, originality shows itself in the interweaving of various strands of interest in the justice preoccupation to give one the sense of a 'texture' rather than a chronicle; but chronicle more or less takes over in the latter part of the novel, where both the interest and the grip slacken. As in other connections, the argument that Scott's inconsistencies can be readily explained by the pressures of the literary market seems to me insufficient, though doubtless they have a relevance. His failures, and the unsatisfactory aspects of relative successes, have all the appearance of resulting from a non-sifting of things which deeply engaged him from those in which his interest was comparatively superficial. To that extent he can really be said to have lacked the critical rigour which, whether or not overtly acknowledged, marks 'the creative writer's interest in literature'.

In the three novels I am going on to consider, Scott is in some respects at his most deeply engaged, and relatively unoriginal in others. That does not mean that parts of them are virtually unreadable, but that what is rewarding in them stands out very sharply from the commonplace. Especially is this true of *Guy Mannering*, in obvious ways an utterly preposterous book. There is the sensational astrological nonsense early on, there are the silly letters of Julia Mannering to her friend Matilda Marchmont, and Scott provides a fair infusion of pretty crude melodrama. Quite often the reader may wonder what has happened to the Scott who satirically tilts at contemporary fictional conventions in Chapter I of *Waverley*. Is he not falling a prey to the same sort of thing himself? The working out of the plot, moreover, so full of coincidence, catastrophe, and seemingly unavoidable disaster, though enjoyable enough at a simple level, is not in itself adequate to sustain interest over more than one reading.

Fortunately *Guy Mannering* exhibits 'working out' of a more intelligently substantial kind. Here one needs to turn to the most

famous single passage in the book: the rhetorical denunciation of
Godfrey Bertram by Meg Merrilies in Chapter 8. Bertram has
ordered the gipsies off his land, and here is Meg's 'proudly contemptuous' farewell:

'Ride your ways,' said the gipsy, 'ride your ways, Laird of Ellangowan;
ride your ways, Godfrey Bertram! This day have ye quenched seven smoking
hearths; see if the fire in your ain parlour burn the blither for that. Ye have
riven the thack off seven cottar houses; look if your ain roof-tree stand the
faster. Ye may stable your stirks in the shealings at Derncleugh; see that the
hare does not couch on the hearthstane at Ellangowan. Ride your ways, Godfrey Bertram; what do ye glower after our folk for? There's thirty hearts there
that wad hae wanted bread ere ye had wanted sunkets, and spent their life-
blood ere ye had scratched your finger. Yes; there's thirty yonder, from the
auld wife of an hundred to the babe that was born last week, that ye have
turned out o' thir bits o' bields, to sleep with the tod and the blackcock in the
muirs! Ride your ways, Ellangowan. Our bairns are hinging at our weary
backs; look that your braw cradle at hame be the fairer spread up; not that I
am wishing ill to little Harry, or to the babe that's yet to be born – God for-
bid – and make them kind to the poor, and better folk than their father!
And now, ride e'en your ways; for these are the last words ye'll ever hear Meg
Merrilies speak, and this is the last reise that I'll ever cut in the bonny woods
of Ellangowan.'

So saying, she broke the sapling she held in her hand, and flung it into the
road.   (49–50)

thack thatch; *stirks* steers; *shealings* huts; *sunkets* delicacies; *bields* shelters; *tod* fox; *muirs* moors; *hinging*
hanging; *braw* fine; *reise* twig, small branch

The passage has been a good deal admired for the almost Shake-
spearian impact of its vernacular energy (for once the comparison
is not wholly out of place), but Meg's tirade has deeper implication than pure 'effect', implications which make us ask just why
she has launched into it. When we try to answer this question, we
find ourselves recognizing *Guy Mannering* as being at any rate
partly preoccupied with the subject of social change. Godfrey
Bertram, as hereditary Laird of Ellangowan, has assumed in the
past the traditional validity of the right of the gipsies, who for
generations have been settlers on the family estate, to remain there,
and to look on the Bertrams, in fact, as their patrons and protec-
tors. Their tradition of settlement there has led to their being
regarded almost 'as proprietors of the wretched shealings which
they inhabited', though from a strictly legal viewpoint they have
had no official rights whatever. The tie between the gipsies and the

family has been of a feudal nature, for the other side of the bargain which has permitted them to live on the estate unmolested is that they have given 'service to the Laird in war, or, more frequently, by infesting or plundering the lands of the neighbouring barons with whom he chanced to be at feud'. Bertram knows all this only too well. As a justice of the peace in a modern non-feudal age, however, he has yielded to pressure to drive these so-called 'vagrants' from the neighbourhood. A relationship existing in no legally official form, but regarded by the gipsies as possessing the sanctity conferred by time, has thus been broken. The informal tradition of the old order has given way to the cold legalism of the new. Meg's breaking of the sapling symbolically sums this up.

Waverley shows the withering-away of the old Highland order, and the assumption of supreme authority by the forces of 'progress', forces set in motion by the Union of 1707. We find also in that novel the virtual end of the ancient Lowland aristocracy, for if the Baron of Bradwardine survives, it is without his former standing. *Guy Mannering*, similarly, shows us the Ellangowan estate, a bastion of the old hereditary gentry, passing into the hands of a new upstart class personified in the corrupt lawyer Gilbert Glossin. The new *parvenus* have the money; the old gentry are without it. With due allowance made for different ways of describing it, the situation is by no means unfamiliar in the Asia and Africa of today.

Scott handles the conflict between the old and new with considerable subtlety. At no time does he sentimentally idealize the gentry in *Guy Mannering*; all in all they are no better than they should be. One may understand Godfrey Bertram's position with regard to the gipsies, but such gestures as his attempting to fob off the enraged Meg Merrilies with a half-crown tip are merely contemptible. Meg on the other hand, who in a different way represents the old way of life, is portrayed with a similar absence of sentimentality. Though she has her own very authentic impressiveness (as the great tirade demonstrates), she does not see herself as a 'good' woman in an orthodox sense, and certainly is not made to come across to the reader as such. And Scott's avoidance of sentimental traps renders his depiction of social change all the

more convincing. Whatever personal weaknesses the characters of
Godfrey Bertram and Meg Merrilies may be shown to suffer from,
they symbolically represent what was once, before Bertram's
eviction of the gipsies, a coherent social order in which gentleman and gipsy could live in a relationship of mutual tolerance and
mutual reliance.

   This, of course, is something that the upstart Gilbert Glossin
simply cannot understand. He has the money, he buys the estate
of Ellangowan, so why should he not be regarded as the laird?
As Fergus Mac-Ivor in *Waverley* is sometimes addressed as
'Glennaquoich', the name of his own patrimonial land, so Glossin
supposes that his purchase of Ellangowan must automatically
earn him the right to the same kind of 'territorial appellation'.
But money cannot buy his being recognized as anything but a
pretender:

And when he looked abroad he could not but be sensible that he was
excluded from the society of the gentry of the country, to whose rank he con-
ceived he had raised himself. He was not admitted to their clubs, and at meet-
ings of a public nature, from which he could not be altogether excluded, he
found himself thwarted and looked upon with coldness and contempt. Both
principle and prejudice co-operated in creating this dislike; for the gentlemen
of the country despised him for the lowness of his birth, while they hated him
for the means by which he had raised his fortune. With the common people
his reputation stood still worse. They would neither yield him the territorial
appellation of Ellangowan nor the usual compliment of Mr. Glossin: with
them he was bare Glossin; and so incredible was his vanity interested by this
trifling circumstance, that he was known to give half-a-crown to a beggar
because he had thrice called him Ellangowan in beseeching him for a penny.
(204-5)

Clearly Scott has no great liking for him; yet, in spite of his turning out to be a villain as well as an upstart, one finds it hard to re-
sist a certain feeling of sympathy for Glossin. Suppose, after all,
that he had *not* been devious and corrupt. Would the social system
have permitted him, no matter how intrinsically worthy he might
have been, to better himself? And is there not something wrong
with a system that would not? Scott obliges us to put those questions by associating Glossin with a phenomenally obtuse specimen
of landed arrogance in the shape of Sir Robert Hazlewood. Each
imagines that he has manipulative control of the other: Glossin

simply because the role is second nature to him, Sir Robert because to his way of thinking superior birth naturally confers superior intelligence. Neither man comes at all well out of the involvement. Glossin is characteristically underhand, while Sir Robert emerges as both ridiculous and hypocritical; for normally his aristocratic pride would make him consider a man like Glossin to be quite beneath his notice, let alone his close association.

The dénouement of the book brings an orthodox apportionment of deserts. With straight poetic justice Glossin meets a villain's end, as does his brutal confederate Dirk Hatteraick. The ousted Bertrams are restored to their ancestral property of Ellangowan, with the long-lost heir Harry Bertram assuming true identity and rightful position, and winning the right woman into the bargain. Everybody, one supposes, lives happily ever after.

But Scott is rather more subtle than that. If the end of *Guy Mannering* offers a scene of well-won stability, the book's overall exhibition of change and insecurity induces a certain scepticism as to its long-term implications. Content we may be to let Bertram and his bride live for years undisturbed, yet the new class that Glossin has represented, the class for which money counts above all things, is not put out of the way by the worsting of one man. Change is inescapable. Future Bertrams, we may speculate, will perhaps have to become equally money-conscious, if not equally unscrupulous. Scott could see these things going on around him. The vaguely eighteenth-century setting of *Guy Mannering* can let us put it very close indeed to his own lifetime: even well within it.

The ambiguity of feeling about *Guy Mannering*'s superficially serene conclusion informs another aspect of this oddly mixed novel, an aspect which links it with *The Heart of Midlothian*. Glossin is a roguish lawyer. Set over against him is the 'good' Mr Pleydell, the honest man of the law as opposed to the devious schemer. That in itself suggests a stage all set for a dramatized debate on legal use and abuse. But whereas in *The Heart of Midlothian* 'poetic justice' does not really begin to figure until after the main debate on the nature of justice is over, in *Guy Mannering* Scott's probings and ponderings on the subject of legal justice are associated throughout with a concern with justice of other kinds, poetic justice included. Though this does not make *Guy Mannering* a better novel than *The Heart of Midlothian*, it does give the book a distinction which acts together with its social-historical strength to save it from being merely stereotyped.

'Poetic justice' is seen most obviously in the fulfilment of the prophecy (see Chapter 41) that

> Bertram's right and Bertram's might
> Shall meet on Ellangowan height.

With triumphant aptness Glossin and Hatteraick are disposed of. Things are now as they should be. True 'justice' has been done. But our sense of this goes with an awareness of justice in other shapes. Hardly any personage in the book avoids being strikingly an agent or recipient of justice or injustice in some form. To take a few instances, there is Mannering's haunted feeling of having been unjust to Brown, and unjust to his own wife; there is the advice of his friend Mervyn, urging him to regard it as 'just' to defend one's reputation; there is Sir Robert Hazlewood's ludicrously class-based notion of justice, according to which the seriousness of an offence is to be gauged in proportion to the social rank of the person who suffers from it; there is Dandie Dinmont's fanatical obsession with seeing that justice is done, as a matter of principle, in a case of almost incredible triviality.

Returning to Godfrey Bertram and his eviction of the gipsies, we find that he has earlier complained bitterly to Mannering about the manifest injustice of his not being made a justice of the peace, and that when at last the honour is conferred upon him, his behaviour to the settlers is dictated by anxiety to belie his old reputation for 'inert good nature'. His harbouring of the gipsies is held against him in his new judicial position. He is accused of hypocrisy in standing up for law and order while at the same time permitting pure 'vagrants' to continue in the neighbourhood. A local political enemy has it that 'while he affected a great zeal for the public police, and seemed ambitious of the fame of an active magistrate, he fostered a tribe of the greatest rogues in the country, and permitted them to harbour within a mile of the house of Ellangowan.' Bertram thus acts 'unjustly' towards the gipsies from their own point of view, because this essentially weak man wishes to be thought a true upholder of 'just' local order. No wonder he has an unquiet conscience when the 'vagrants' depart:

His sensations were bitter enough. The race, it is true, which he had thus summarily dismissed from their ancient place of refuge, was idle and vicious; but had he endeavoured to render them otherwise? They were not more irregular characters now than they had been while they were admitted to consider themselves as a sort of subordinate dependents of his family; and ought the mere circumstance of his becoming a magistrate to have made at once such a change in his conduct towards them? Some means of reformation ought at least to have been tried before sending seven families at once upon the wide world, and depriving them of a degree of countenance which withheld them at least from atrocious guilt. (48–9)

A weak man's crude assertion of conspicuous strength as justice of the peace has thus led to a conflict within him between the comfortable thought that he is doing the legally 'right' thing in driving the settlers away, and the totally discomforting sense that from a truly human standpoint he is being thoroughly unjust.

Meg Merrilies speaks in the name of purely 'human' justice (very close to that of the Edinburgh mob in *The Heart of Midlothian*) when she launches into her great tirade, aptly following close upon the passage which reveals Bertram's uneasy conscience. One must understand the full extent of her outrage. For it comes not only from bitterness at having to leave an apparently secure anchorage, but also from the appalling reversal of the values she has hitherto unquestioningly associated with the house of Ellangowan. Bertram has seemed to her at once a worthy representative of his aristocratic line and an embodiment of that 'human' feeling for justice he has now outwardly repudiated: 'a real gentleman for sae mony hundred years, and never hunds puir fowk aff your grund as if they were mad tykes'. And it is precisely because his past treatment of the gipsies has forged a bond of loyalty to the family, despite their subsequent suffering at his hands, that Meg is so shocked at the news that Ellangowan has been sold after his death, and to Glossin of all people:

'Sell'd!' echoed the gipsy, with something like a scream; 'and wha durst buy Ellangowan that was not of Bertram's blude? and wha could tell whether

76

the bonny knave-bairn may not come back to claim his ain? wha durst buy
the estate and the castle of Ellangowan?'
  'Troth, gudewife, just ane o' thae writer chields that buys a' thing; they
ca' him Glossin, I think.'
  'Glossin! Gibbie Glossin! that I have carried in my creels a hundred
times, for his mother wasna muckle better than mysell – he to presume to buy
the barony of Ellangowan! Gude be wi' us; it is an awfu' warld! I wished him
ill; but no sic a downfa' as a' that neither. Wae's me! wae's me to think o't!
. . . It will be seen and heard of – earth and sea will not hold their peace
langer!' (142–3)

blude blood; *knave-bairn* boy-child; *wha* who; *chields* fellows; *creels* baskets; *muckle* much; *warld* world;
wae woe; *langer* longer

Meg's sense of what is 'just', instinctively human in response to
Ellangowan's downfall, is here linked with her conviction of what
is socially just (that Ellangowan must be in the right hands) and
with an extra-human 'justice' which she feels must be exercised
by the elements themselves in protest against so shocking a viola-
tion of the fitness of things. And from now on this woman who in
obvious ways is a figure quite 'outside the law' will be a major
contributor to the process whereby 'justice is done' in the strictly
legal sense, as well as in the human sense where 'justice' is based
on old sentiments, traditional loyalties, and the belief in an abiding
natural order.

  Meg's counterpart on the plane of the law, likewise contributing
to the downfall of Glossin and the restoration of the Bertrams, is
Mr Counsellor Pleydell. He gives Scott the opportunity for a
lively picture of the lighter side of eighteenth-century legal
Edinburgh, but the circumstances in which the surprised Mannering first finds him do more than provide us with an exuberant
interlude (see Chapter 36). To Mr Pleydell Saturday night is
sacrosanct; the law is laid aside, frolic prevails. In one way, of
course, this introduces him to the reader as an eminently 'human'
person, who will cheerfully play the fool when off duty, while not
being any the less astute when the high jinks are over. Certainly he
reveals himself as not only human but 'humane', when, making
an exception in his Saturday-night rule for the sake of Mannering,
he reacts with instant sympathy to mention of Lucy Bertram. But
in quite another manner Mr Pleydell's first appearance, when one
looks back on it, strengthens the overall impression that, whatever

his virtues, he is a *professional* to his fingertips. Who but the most deeply dyed professional, one asks, would with such conscious rigour, in positively extreme terms, separate out his legal week from his merrymaking Saturday?

Now it would be stupidly perverse to make an adverse critical point about Mr Pleydell's professionalism. Without it Harry Bertram would be nowhere, and Glossin would reign triumphant. What I am trying to suggest may best be brought home by comparing him with a third legal figure in *Guy Mannering* – Mr Mac-Morlan. Here, to be sure, is a man of unimpeachable honesty and humanity. Yet although one attributes those same virtues to Mr Pleydell, one recognizes in his professional make-up something that Mac-Morlan is entirely without: a worldly-wise cynicism. A 'good' lawyer Mr Pleydell really is, in the sense in which one speaks of a 'good' man. On the other hand he knows full well that in another sense a 'good' lawyer can be simply an adroit legal scoundrel. Mr. Pleydell comes nowhere remotely near being that, but in Chapter 56 he cannot help revealing to Mannering his admiration for the cleverness of Glossin, that fully-rounded specimen of a 'good' lawyer in the bad sense: 'I can tell you Glossin would have been a pretty lawyer had he not had such a turn for the roguish part of the profession.' Just because he is such a professional, Mr Pleydell has no illusions about the law. 'Law's like laudanum,' he remarks in one place; 'it's much more easy to use it as a quack does than to learn to apply it like a physician.'

Scott no more intends here to undermine belief in the law than he does in *The Heart of Midlothian*; the author of *Waverley* was no anarchist. But *Guy Mannering* reminds us that the law may quite readily be used for ends which are anything but the ends of justice, its provisions becoming mere currency for inhuman professional speculation. Moreover, in the working of Mr Counsellor Pleydell and the wandering Meg Merrilies toward the same doing of justice, we see symbolically expressed an alliance of the strictly 'legal' and the emotionally 'human', an alliance which acts as a safeguard against the unscrupulously adroit. Neither way of looking at justice can properly do its job without the other.

Civilized man needs both of them, always and everywhere.

I have not aimed at comprehensiveness in discussing *Guy Mannering*. The book's inconsistencies of quality would hardly have made comprehensiveness desirable. One cannot neatly disentangle all that it exhibits of strength from relatively inferior surrounding matter, a fact which renders it highly characteristic of Scott, and makes discriminating perseverance on the reader's part especially necessary. For one would not wish to be without the novel's counterpointing of different views of justice, or that aspect of it which is imaginative social history. (The treatment of Dandie Dinmont, amongst the figures I have not concentrated on, repays attention where Scott the social historian is in question.) *Redgauntlet* likewise offers things one would not be without, 'Wandering Willie's Tale' above all. Yet although what is best in the book is richer than the equivalent in *Guy Mannering*, it has damaging weaknesses.

Since this study hopes to encourage interest in Scott, my focus will be the *strength* of *Redgauntlet*. The weaknesses cannot, however, simply be wished away, and the book's cause may be furthered if they are briefly confronted for what they are. Chief among them, and here even old-style enthusiasm for Scott largely agrees, is the ineptitude of the early chapters. What one can only call the mutual epistolary back-scratchings of the two friends, Darsie Latimer and Alan Fairford, are a bore and an embarrassment. The book is far too long in getting off the ground. Only when the epistolary form begins to take on the flavour of third-person narrative does life really start to flow. Then there is the due ingredient, as in *Guy Mannering*, of the heir who comes to know his true identity: Darsie Latimer, transmogrified into Sir Arthur Darsie Redgauntlet. The plot cannot do without this item of stock, so it has to be put up with. Similarly the tiresome mystification surrounding 'Green Mantle', for whom Darsie conceives a romantic attachment, only to find that she is his sister Lilias. (Happily Fairford is available to her as a husband.) All these things come from that side of Scott which is least engaged and thus least enterprising.

Where, then, does *Redgauntlet* manifest real engagement?

Superficially the book resembles *Waverley*, in that it has at the centre a Jacobite conspiracy, though this time a fictitious one, and one which never flares into actual fighting. Suppose, Scott asks, there had been an attempt later in the eighteenth century to revive the spirit of the 1745 Rebellion. What kind of man would have been involved? What would have been the prospects for success? What forces would have militated against it? The existence of *Waverley* is enough to tell us that Scott's attention to such questions will not be perfunctory.

During the ten years or so between the writing of these two books, Scott's attitude towards the Jacobite cause has hardened somewhat. If *Waverley* can hardly be called pro-Jacobite in overall effect, the cause and its implications do quite often evoke a sympathetic response, whatever the qualifications. In *Redgauntlet*, though elements of sympathy can still be found in places, qualification has turned into something more like downright censure, verging at times on ridicule. One would never think of Flora Mac-Ivor as an absurd figure; Redgauntlet, on the other hand, can come quite close to being one.

Not for nothing does he give the book its title. His fanaticism, often ostentatiously melodramatic in expression, symbolically embodies what Scott sees as the central weakness of this new conspiracy: its anachronistic futility. The country does not *need* the Stuarts; to seek their restoration is to turn the clock back, to plunge the land into meaningless chaos. Yet to do this is Redgauntlet's obsession. If he frequently seems 'unreal' in his frowning outbursts, the effect is deliberate. The whole notion of a second '45 *is* unreal.

But Scott's interest in the idea of a revived conspiracy expresses itself not only in censure, overt or implied; there is also a very real awareness of the danger men like Redgauntlet represent, doomed to failure though they be from the start. I say 'very *real* awareness' with special point, for while Redgauntlet's fanaticism comes across to us as 'unreal', the dangers of social disorder inherent in his kind of irresponsibility are 'real' indeed. Looked at with this in mind, the book becomes another examination of justice and law, with a dimension we have not met so far. *The Heart of Midlothian* and

Guy Mannering warn us against taking legal justice for granted, at the same time showing us that other conceptions of justice exist. *Redgauntlet* goes further: it urges us to beware of taking for granted not only justice of any kind, but the whole assumption of law and order upon which civilized society rests. Precisely because he is so committed to law and order does Scott here show them in danger of breaking down. One need hardly point out how permanently relevant that is.

Our sense of Redgauntlet himself as the epitome of the forces making for breakdown arises both from his own literal statements and from the book's bold handling of symbolism. Consider the use of the deadly Solway tide, to which Darsie Latimer nearly falls victim on two occasions. On the simplest level the Solway is the dividing line between Scotland, where Darsie is safe, and the England upon whose soil he has been warned not to set foot, the treacherous tide being thus a symbolic reminder of the dangers awaiting him on the English shore, where he will be at Redgauntlet's mercy. But there is more to it than that. The tide rushes up the estuary with lethal speed, yet Redgauntlet himself, though abundantly aware of its perils, seems quite at home with it. And it is no accident that this should be so, for both Redgauntlet and the tide pursue their courses with a common impetuosity and ruthlessness once they have begun. Both sweep everything before them. Redgauntlet has no more respect for the law (though he may cynically use it when it suits his purpose) than has the mighty onrush of water.

Justice, in the legal sense, is a matter of no import to Redgauntlet. The only kind of secular justice that has any meaning to him is the justice, as he sees it, of the Stuart cause. Although he speaks feelingly of the days 'when Scotland was herself, and had her own King and Legislature', one's impression is that even the law of pre-Union Scotland would have meant little to him. And if he does not believe in law, it is because he does not believe in freedom. In Chapter 8, from which the words just quoted are taken, Darsie, who is in his hands, claims 'the privilege of acting for myself', and declares 'constraint shall not deprive me of an Englishman's best privilege'. Redgauntlet's response makes short work of what he calls 'the true cant of the day':

'The privilege of free action belongs to no mortal; we are tied down by the fetters of duty, our mortal path is limited by the regulations of honour, our most indifferent actions are but meshes of the web of destiny by which we are all surrounded . . . Yes, young man, in doing and suffering we play but the part allotted by Destiny, the manager of this strange drama, stand bound to act no more than is prescribed, to say no more than is set down for us; and yet we mouth about free-will, and freedom of thought and action, as if Richard must not die, or Richmond conquer, exactly where the author has decreed it shall be so!' (223–4)

Not only does Redgauntlet's outburst, thoroughly typical in its hectoring extravagance, deny the reality of free-will; it also jumbles together duty, honour, and destiny, in a wild confusion. The man is not a lunatic, but his words manifest a total disregard for reason and distinction parallel to his contempt for legal justice. Justice, for him, is justice meted out by destiny, justice as inexorable as that to which Shakespeare brings Richard III, justice as relentless as the careering Solway tide.

Since the novel bears Redgauntlet's name, it is not surprising that its general flavour should be characterized by an overall impression of law and order, and the justice associated with them, either breaking down or threatening to do so. The sense of judicial breakdown arises most specifically from the extraordinary imprisonment to which Darsie is subjected by Redgauntlet (who turns out to be his uncle), a restraint at which a *bona fide*, if fatuous, magistrate connives. But it is also associated with a whole series of characters who are, in one way or another, 'outside the law'. This sort of world, we come to feel, makes it quite to be expected that Darsie's protest that his detention is illegal and 'highly punishable by the laws which protect the liberties of the subject' should be uttered in vain. There is, for example, Nanty Ewart, an amiable drunk, 'who, by his own account, had been a pirate, and who was at present, in all probability, an outlaw as well as a contraband trader'; there is the pseudo-pious cleric Thomas Trumbull, who appears superficially to be very much within the law, but whose speciality, apart from smuggling, is the dissemination of pornography; there is the youthful delinquent, little Benjie; there is, for that matter, Wandering Willie the fiddler, not engaged in strikingly illicit activities, but living a life, as his name suggests, that is essentially a law unto itself. Finally there is Prince Charles Edward, somewhat battered since his appearance in *Waverley*, together with those who seek to put him on the throne.

Directly opposed to everything those characters stand for in the book's organization, is legal Edinburgh, with the punctilious Mr Fairford as its chief representative. Whatever his virtues, Saunders Fairford is no Mr Pleydell; his brand of legal professionalism, though eminently honest and dogged, is totally unadorned with the graces of urbanity. And indeed the law in this novel, though Alan Fairford applies himself to his father's profession with a tolerably good grace and with considerable promise, hardly shines out as a beacon of civilized enlightenment. The case in which Alan at first makes so good an impression, for example, is the notorious affair of a preposterous drunkard, Peter Peebles. This outrageous creature provides a deal of amusement (as a comic figure he is genuinely funny, unlike the tiresome Dominie Sampson in *Guy Mannering*), but Alan's professional plea for him as 'a victim to protracted justice, and to the hope delayed which sickens the heart' awakens in the reader, as distinct from the Bench, only a very little sympathy, so rapacious a waster is he. Even the severely limited sympathy we may once have felt is quite swept away by the lies he tells when in pursuit of Alan later in the book – Alan having gone in search of his friend Darsie, whom Redgauntlet is trying to force into the conspiracy. Peebles affords, in fact, a good example of the book's way of arousing suspended judgements. We find ourselves uncertain whether he really is a sad victim of the law's delay, in which case his disreputable behaviour has some measure of excuse, or whether he is so fundamentally appalling a person that his failure to get a judgement in his favour is actually richly deserved. 'Evidence', one way or the other, is offered from time to time, but we can never be quite sure what to think and are tempted to conclude that the fairest thing is simply to pronounce him crazy and leave it at that. All in all his association in the book with courts and legal figures serves to surround the law with a certain atmosphere of seediness and futility. If *this* is the law, no wonder Redgauntlet holds it in such contempt.

The uncertain or suspended judgement typifies this novel. About some characters (Thomas Trumbull, for instance, or the treacherous Cristal Nixon) one is in no doubt. A person like the seemingly admirable Quaker, Joshua Geddes, on the other hand, is a problem. One can indicate the nature of this by remarking that to call him only 'seemingly admirable' immediately poses a question of fairness. Has one any good reason for suspecting that the tranquil ways of this worthy man, visibly symbolized by the order in which he keeps his property, conceal anything which might be described as hypocrisy? Surely not: though one cannot help reflecting that in Mr Geddes strict principle is not incompatible with material prosperity. Then there is this passage from letter 7, in which his sister is showing Darsie round the grounds, which, 'though not extensive, might rival an earl's in point of care and expense':

Rachel carried me first to her own favourite resort, a poultry-yard, stocked with a variety of domestic fowls, of the more rare as well as the most ordinary kinds, furnished with every accommodation which may suit their various habits . . .

All these creatures seemed to recognise the presence of their mistress, and some especial favourites hastened to her feet, and continued to follow her as far as their limits permitted. She pointed out their peculiarities and qualities, with the discrimination of one who had made natural history her study; and I own I never looked on barn-door fowls with so much interest before – at least until they were boiled or roasted. I could not help asking the trying question, how she could order the execution of any of the creatures of which she seemed so careful.

'It was painful,' she said, 'but it was according to the law of their being. They must die; but they knew not when death was approaching; and in making them comfortable while they lived, we contributed to their happiness as much as the conditions of their existence permitted to us.'

I am not quite of her mind, Alan. I do not believe either pigs or poultry would admit that the chief end of their being was to be killed and eaten. However, I did not press the argument, from which my Quaker seemed rather desirous to escape. (67–8)

Note that last touch, so characteristic of this novel. Whence the good lady's desire to change the subject? Does it come from humane sorrow at the doleful necessity of killing for the table? Or does it spring from an uncomfortable awareness that her argument is too glib to stand further pursuit? We are most certainly not encouraged in any way to dislike Mr Geddes or his sister. It is simply that rather awkward questions arise when one looks at the pair as embodiments of law and order governed by strict though not ferocious religious principle. They can hardly be called puritanical bigots, yet one may have the nagging sense that somehow, somewhere, there is something 'wrong' with them.

Consider the main cause of conflict between Mr Geddes and Redgauntlet, the outcome of which enables the latter to kidnap his nephew and carry him off to England. Redgauntlet is a sportsman, for whom the hunting of fish in the Solway is as much a recreation as a way of obtaining food. For Mr Geddes, however, there is no thought of sport; the obtaining of the fish is an object in itself, according to which principle he erects traps to snare them. To the enraged Redgauntlet there is one remedy: destroy the traps.

Now in one way Redgauntlet is clearly in the wrong for creating a breach of the peace by his attack; but sympathy for Mr Geddes is a little qualified. Are his fish-traps tolerable, from the point of view of strict legality or even of plain human fairness to others? Is the attack on them actually 'unjust', or is it a case of equivocal 'justice', like Godfrey Bertram's eviction of the gipsies from Ellangowan, with the balance of favour perhaps falling to Redgauntlet?

Awkward questions such as those (and many more could be asked, in connection with other characters) are a preparation, as the reader eventually sees, for the book's extraordinary climax. This climax, or anti-climax, may give one the feeling of having been cheated. A deal of suspense and mystery has been built up, the narrative seems to be sweeping to a grand explosion of violence, and what happens? There are the violent deaths of Nanty Ewart and Cristal Nixon, which respectively awaken compassion and satisfy a straightforward desire for 'poetic justice'; but, as far as Redgauntlet and the prince are concerned, the story just fizzles out.

In fact this ending is thoroughly in keeping with the tone of the novel as a whole. Almost everywhere we turn there is breakdown, both in the prevailing atmosphere of lawlessness and in the 'government' of the individual person's life. Both Nanty Ewart and Peter Peebles are to different extents human wrecks. Thomas

Trumbull is a moral wreck, and well on the way to being a physical one to boot. The prince himself is a man in premature physical decay, whose private morals will not stand close inspection. Events often carry with them similar implications. The hearing of the Peebles case breaks down when Alan learns of his friend's peril and hurries off. The tranquil existence of the Geddes couple is shattered by violence. Even 'Wandering Willie's Tale', in which the frontier between reality and fantasy is broken down with a vengeance, is seen by the teller as having had sadly disruptive consequences for his own life.

The conspiracy likewise breaks down. From the government's point of view, of course, and essentially from the author's, that is a 'just' conclusion. Indeed, it may be urged that Redgauntlet and the prince receive more than justice when General Campbell allows them to depart unharmed.

The thoughtful reader, however, will not find it easy to rest content with so simple a view, or to suppose that Scott means us to see the matter in that way alone. A consideration of both the actual scene before the prince in the makeshift presence chamber, and the discussion which precedes it, makes definite judgement exceedingly difficult. The conspirators are in so appallingly difficult a position themselves that although we may from time to time feel admiration for some or contempt for others, we cannot for long persist in a clear-cut view of them – except in the case of Redgauntlet, who is likely to retain the reader's qualified admiration for his selfless devotion, dangerously irresponsible though we know him to be. Take this passage from Chapter 22; Redgauntlet has just announced that 'Charles Edward is in this country – Charles Edward is in this house!' to the gathering of conspirators who have expected nothing but a 'consultation':

There was a deep pause. Those among the conspirators whom mere habit or a desire of preserving consistency had engaged in the affair now saw with terror their retreat cut off; and others, who at a distance had regarded the proposed enterprise as hopeful, trembled when the moment of actually embarking in it was thus unexpectedly and almost inevitably precipitated.

'How now, my lords and gentlemen!' said Redgauntlet. 'Is it delight and rapture that keep you thus silent? Where are the eager welcomes that should be paid to your rightful king, who a second time confides his person to the care of his subjects, undeterred by the hairbreadth escapes and severe privations of his former expedition? I hope there is no gentleman here that is not ready to redeem, in his prince's presence, the pledge of fidelity which he offered in his absence?'

'I, at least,' said the young nobleman, resolutely, and laying his hand on his sword, 'will not be that coward. If Charles is come to these shores, I will be the first to give him welcome, and to devote my life and fortune to his service.'

'Before Cot,' said Mr. Meredith, 'I do not see that Mr. Redgauntlet has left us anything else to do.'

'Stay,' said Summertrees, 'there is yet another question. Has he brought any of those Irish rapparees with him, who broke the neck of our last glorious affair?'

'Not a man of them,' said Redgauntlet.

'I trust,' said Dr. Grumball, 'that there are no Catholic priests in his company? I would not intrude on the private conscience of my sovereign, but, as an unworthy son of the Church of England, it is my duty to consider her security.'   (399–400)

rapparees plunderers, good-for-nothings

And so the inquisition goes on, most of the prince's 'champions' trying to fasten on him some misdemeanour which will give them an excuse to back out. No wonder Redgauntlet sardonically comments that Charles Edward 'hath but a frozen reception!'

The conspirators may well seem guilty of shocking injustice towards the prince, whatever the wider implications of the projected rebellion. But the very consideration which finally gives them their excuse is precisely the one which makes us think again. Charles Edward has contracted a liaison with a woman regarded as potentially treacherous. By persisting in this relationship he is actually guilty of injustice towards *them*. There is consequently quite 'just' sense in Sir Richard Glendale's declaration that he will see the prince safely to his departing ship and defend him against any possible attack on the way to it, but that once the sails are spread he will take immediate measures for his own protection, surrendering himself if necessary to a justice of peace, and giving security that he will thenceforward 'live quiet, and submit to the ruling powers'.

What, then, has defeated the conspiracy from within, and shown up Redgauntlet as a melodramatic anachronism? Is it simply admirable common sense? Is it merely contemptible self-

87

interest? Or is it that halfway house between the two, which we call "prudence"? Scott could certainly not have countenanced even the temporary success of this fictitious affair, but he leaves us with a rather bitter flavour in the mouth. It is good, no doubt, to see the under-surface grumblings of disorder silenced; but what do we really think of the forces making for order?

I shall return to Scott's interest in the prudential in my next chapter. Meanwhile, *The Antiquary* confronts us with a case of 'mixture' apparently quite unlike *Guy Mannering* or *Redgauntlet*. To say that those two novels are 'mixed' is to suggest the co-existence in them of strikingly contrasted strength and weakness, and to imply the need for the reader boldly to discriminate. Yet what is strong in the books comes out clearly in coherent patterns of interest. If one could wish certain things away, one still has no doubt as to where each work, at its best, is 'going'.

With *The Antiquary* the problem is to find any principle of real coherence at all, beyond the mechanics of the plot – which again involves the ennoblement of a young man seemingly obscure. Scott himself had a special affection for this novel, which perhaps explains why some modern critics have tried so very hard to see it as a whole, not invariably with success. I shall propose a way of looking at it as a unity, a way which I hope is unstrained and clear of special pleading, but as an introduction to this it may be useful briefly to glance at some other opinions.

In a useful book on the Scottish Waverley Novels, *Under Which King?* (Edinburgh, 1969), Robert C. Gordon closes his third chapter with these words: '*The Antiquary* is a very odd novel.' Indeed it is, and he tabulates with exemplary clarity the book's 'instances where "heterogeneous elements are yoked by violence together"', and its 'discordant juxtapositions and "purposes mistook"'. An important clue to its strange individual character, a clue to which I shall come back, is contained in Gordon's view of the particular *kind* of heterogeneity the work exhibits: 'These anti-climaxes, dissonances, obscurities suggest a sort of careless mannerism, as though Scott were mocking the whole idea of coherence and perspective.' And he remarks on a declining coherence of design 'in the conventional sense' through the first three novels (*Waverley, Guy Mannering, The Antiquary*), observing that 'It would seem that the closer Scott came to his own age the more chaotic the world became for him.' These are most useful perceptions, but Gordon's treatment of the book as a whole does not seem to me quite to satisfy a sense that *The Antiquary* has a principle of coherence going beyond its abundance of incongruities.

Another way of looking at the novel comes from David Daiches, in his essay 'Scott's Achievement as a Novelist' (reprinted in *Modern Judgements: Walter Scott*). For him *The Antiquary* presents no real problem of coherence at all. Its 'prevailing atmosphere', he tells us, 'is comic', and although 'The melodramatic Glenallan episode in this novel and the drowning of the young fisherman Steenie Mucklebackit give a sense of depth and implication to the action,...they do not alter its essential atmosphere.' No one is likely to query any contention that the book has a deal of comedy in it, but to claim the comic as its 'prevailing atmosphere' is another matter. Is it enough to 'fit in' melodramatic or tragic elements merely by saying that they 'give a sense of depth and implication'? 'Implication' of *what*? And although I agree with another remark of Daiches that the plot of *The Antiquary* hardly counts in itself, I cannot accept his view that it is 'essentially a static novel', since the heterogeneities to which Gordon rightly points engender shocks and surprises in the reader quite inconsistent with any notion of stasis.

Edgar Johnson in his massive biographical and critical study, *Sir Walter Scott: The Great Unknown* (London, 1970), makes *The Antiquary* seem a more unified thing than does Gordon, whilst at the same time he is far more aware than Daiches of its heterogeneity. Though he does not consider the work to be flawless, his overall judgement is that 'Far from being a cluttered ragbag of a story, like Oldbuck's study and his historical lore, the novel when truly understood is seen to have the clearest thematic unity.' And for him that unity lies in the book's exploration of 'the way in which the present is rooted in the past', and in its rectification of 'the errors of that present by putting it into a sound relationship with the past'. But although that is no doubt true of *The Antiquary*, as it is of many novels, and not only Scott's, Johnson does not really strike me as getting to the heart of the book's heterogeneity. The kind of 'thematic unity' proposed does plausibly explain the *presence* of many heterogeneous elements; it does not, however, do much to account for their *effect*.

I suggest that *The Antiquary*, if not 'a cluttered ragbag', is a very conscious compilation of incongruities. The antiquary himself, known variously as Oldbuck and Monkbarns (the latter being the name of his property), who is plainly an ironic self-portrait, to some extent, of the author in his more extravagantly antiquarian guise, stands in the centre of a whole social spectrum, from the proud (though absurd) Sir Arthur Wardour to the equally proud (though far from absurd) wandering Edie Ochiltree. Variety, and sometimes outrageously grotesque incongruity, are constantly emphasized. Here, for example, is the appearance of Mr Oldbuck's sister Griselda, in Chapter 6:

> The elderly lady rustled in silks and satins, and bore upon her head a structure resembling the fashion in the ladies' memorandum-book for the year 1770, a superb piece of architecture not much less than a modern Gothic castle, of which the curls might represent the turrets, the black pins the *chevaux de frize*, and the lappets the banners.
>
> The face which, like that of the ancient statues of Vesta, was thus crowned with towers, was large and long, and peaked at nose and chin, and bore in other respects such a ludicrous resemblance to the physiognomy of Mr. Jonathan Oldbuck that Lovel, had they not appeared at once, like Sebastian and Viola in the last scene of the 'Twelfth Night,' might have supposed that the figure before him was his old friend masquerading in female attire. (45–6)

Just as oddly 'miscellaneous' in its own way as that passage, or the description of Mr Oldbuck's study in Chapter 3, is the book's very opening:

> It was early on a fine summer's day, near the end of the eighteenth century, when a young man of genteel appearance, journeying towards the north-east of Scotland, provided himself with a ticket in one of those public carriages which travel between Edinburgh and the Queensferry, at which place, as the name implies, and as is well known to all my northern readers, there is a passage-boat for crossing the Firth of Forth. The coach was calculated to carry six regular passengers, besides such interlopers as the coachman could pick up by the way and intrude upon those who were legally in possession. The tickets which conferred right to a seat in this vehicle of little ease were

dispensed by a sharp-looking old dame, with a pair of spectacles on a very thin nose, who inhabited a 'laigh shop', *anglicè*, a cellar, opening to the High Street by a strait and steep stair, at the bottom of which she sold tape, thread, needles, skeans of worsted, coarse linen cloth, and such feminine gear, to those who had the courage and skill to descend to the profundity of her dwelling without falling headlong themselves or throwing down any of the numerous articles which, piled on each side of the descent, indicated the profession of the trader below.

The tone of the first sentence has a stilted, even pedantic formality, carried on for a moment by '*calculated* to carry six *regular* passengers', and then abruptly disturbed by 'such interlopers as the coachman could *pick up by the way*'. The air of walking on stilts returns with 'The tickets which *conferred right* to a seat', and indeed persists through the whole long sentence which those words open, but it assorts ludicrously with the description of the old dame's shop, which in itself is something of a 'ragbag'.

That is far from being the only instance in *The Antiquary* of a type of prose which in Scott's worst novels would be offered 'straight', but which here very often has its orotundity held up for our amusement by warring elements. Consider this piece of laboured 'fine writing' in Chapter 7, when Sir Arthur and Miss Wardour are walking by the sea:

The sun was now resting his huge disk upon the edge of the level ocean, and gilded the accumulation of towering clouds through which he had travelled the livelong day, and which now assembled on all sides, like misfortunes and disasters around a sinking empire and falling monarch. Still, however, his dying splendour gave a sombre magnificence to the massive congregation of vapours, forming out of their unsubstantial gloom the show of pyramids and towers, some touched with gold, some with purple, some with a hue of deep and dark red. The distant sea, stretched beneath this varied and gorgeous canopy, lay almost portentously still, reflecting back the dazzling and level beams of the descending luminary, and the splendid colouring of the clouds amidst which he was setting. Nearer to the beach, the tide rippled onward in waves of sparkling silver, that imperceptibly, yet rapidly, gained upon the sand.

 With a mind employed in admiration of the romantic scene, or perhaps on some more agitating topic, Miss Wardour advanced in silence by her father's side, whose recently offended dignity did not stoop to open any conversation.

(59)

Not only does that last touch, a reference to a ridiculous argument which has just taken place between Sir Arthur and Mr Oldbuck, doing little credit to either, immediately qualify any feeling that Scott means us to take the romantic splendour over-seriously; we shortly find both Sir Arthur's pretensions and the whole gorgeous panoply cut down to size, when the pair are in peril of drowning and the evening has turned to frightful storm. Edie Ochiltree, who has tried to save them from their predicament only to share it, makes the appropriate comment:

'Good man,' said Sir Arthur, 'can you think of nothing? – of no help? I'll make you rich; I'll give you a farm; I'll – '
'Our riches will be soon equal,' said the beggar, looking out upon the strife of the waters; 'they be sae already, for I hae nae land, and you would give your fair bounds and barony for a square yard of rock that would be dry for twal hours.' (63)

Vanity of vanities, indeed.

To say that is to put the whole meretricious passage about the sunset ('descending luminary') in its place in the economy of *The Antiquary*, and at the same time to indicate why a characterization of the book's 'prevailing atmosphere' as 'comic' will hardly do. The spectacle of Sir Arthur's pride brought low by danger has its comic side, to be sure, but there is the strong likelihood of a wasteful human disaster just round the corner. The drowning of Steenie Mucklebackit, later on, is wasteful disaster not round the corner but there for all to contemplate. And while one can urge the stock reflections about the recognized perils of the fisherman's existence, this particular death seems especially gratuitous. To ask 'Why does it have to happen?' and blame Scott for inserting the disaster for no good reason, is to miss the point. The drowning is there in the novel as an instance, on the starkest level, of one kind of vanity: the vanity of supposing that such deaths should *not* be gratuitous. Equally vain is the endeavour of old Mucklebackit the bereaved father, in Chapter 36, to repair the boat, until 'his feelings appeared altogether to derange the power of attention necessary for his work', and 'he flung his hammer against the boat, as if she had been the intentional cause of his misfortune'.

Vain, too, is Mr Oldbuck's attempt to comfort Mucklebackit and vain likewise, given the circumstances, his cherished belief in stoic fortitude, but the end of this encounter has a further interest: its connection with another 'tragedy', but one on a different level:

> Oldbuck, beaten from the pride of his affected cynicism, would not willingly have had any one by upon that occasion to quote to him his favourite maxims of the Stoic philosophy. The large drops fell fast from his own eyes as he begged the father, who was now melted at recollecting the bravery and generous sentiments of his son, to forbear useless sorrow, and led him by the arm towards his own home, where another scene awaited our Antiquary. As he entered, the first person whom he beheld was Lord Glenallan. (309)

From the stark tragedy of the fisherfolk we come face to face with the melodramatic bag of tricks which is the Glenallan affair. There has, of course, been human suffering involved in it, yet how needless, how essentially futile; and the juxtaposition of this with the Mucklebackit episode is most telling. Scott's concern in this book with the vanity of human wishes and expectations manifests itself on a variety of levels. If the Mucklebackits stand at the lower end of the purely social scale, they are at the top of Scott's scale of seriousness. The Glenallan story, by contrast, is well on the way down.

Vanity exhibits its wastes and its follies all over *The Antiquary*. At the level of the contemptibly absurd we see it in the farcical gulling of Sir Arthur Wardour by the trickster Dousterswivel, who promises him an easy way to wealth. Vain in a gentler style are Mr Oldbuck's sillier antiquarian convictions, in which theory takes over from common sense. And Hector M'Intyre is a prime devotee of the blusteringly vain, both in his touchy pride and in his partiality for useless bravado. A great many more instances could easily be recalled.

To speak of the Vanity of Human Wishes is to be reminded that Scott greatly admired Samuel Johnson's poem of that name. It would be perverse to maintain that *The Antiquary* is all in all a gloomy novel, but that it has a persistently underlying sombre note cannot be doubted if one sees Scott's parading of human vanity in the light of the following: (Mr Oldbuck is speaking to Lovel)

'Be comforted: to have lost a friend by death while your mutual regard was warm and unchilled, while the tear can drop unembittered by any painful recollection of coldness or distrust or treachery, is perhaps an escape from a more heavy dispensation. Look around you; how few do you see grow old in the affections of those with whom their early friendships were formed! Our sources of common pleasure gradually dry up as we journey on through the vale of Bacha, and we hew out to ourselves other reservoirs, from which the first companions of our pilgrimage are excluded; jealousies, rivalries, envy, intervene to separate others from our side, until none remain but those who are connnected with us rather by habit than by predilection, or who, allied more in blood than in disposition, only keep the old man company in his life that they may not be forgotten at his death – ' (140-1)

Not merely are the sentiments typical of Johnson in his darker vein; the very cadences are Johnsonian. Compare the passage with this characteristic piece of pondering on human vanity:

To take a view at once distinct and comprehensive of human life, with all its intricacies of combination, and varieties of connexion, is beyond the power of mortal intelligences. Of the state with which practice has not acquainted us we snatch a glimpse, we discern a point, and regulate the rest by passion, and by fancy. In this inquiry every favourite prejudice, every innate desire, is busy to deceive us. We are unhappy, at least less happy than our nature seems to admit; we necessarily desire the melioration of our lot; what we desire we very reasonably seek, and what we seek we are naturally eager to believe that we have found. Our confidence is often disappointed, but our reason is not convinced, and there is no man who does not hope for something which he has not, though perhaps his wishes lie unactive, because he foresees the difficulty of attainment. (Samuel Johnson, *The Rambler* (23 October 1750))

But as well as Dr Johnson and the eighteenth century, *The Antiquary* looks back to the seventeenth century and the author of *The Alchemist*. Not for nothing does Scott quote from that play at the head of Chapter 23 and again at the end of the same chapter, for Dousterswivel's gulling of Sir Arthur, at this point the topic of concern, could have come out of Ben Jonson. Scott overdoes the farce, as he overplays the baron's pedantry in *Waverley*, but he is certainly aiming for something of a Jonsonian effect. And Ben Jonson's influence is not confined to this strand in the book's texture. We can find it in the idiosyncratic ladies we encounter at the Fairport post office in Chapter 15 – Mrs Mailsetter, Mrs Shortcake, and Mrs Heukbane (the last named being the butcher's wife!). Scott's use of the highly idiosyncratic character, indeed, whether one who is by name quite frankly identified with a particular trade like the three women just mentioned, or one

dominated by some quirk, foible, or outlandish obsession, like
Mr Oldbuck or Sir Arthur Wardour, places him in a central
literary line. Starting from the personified virtues, vices, and
other representative type-figures of the morality plays, it leads
through the 'Humour' characters of Ben Jonson (personages more
apparently realistic than the Morality types, but still representa-
tively embodying common human traits), to Scott's Baron of
Bradwardine, Mr Oldbuck, and many others, and from Scott to
Dickens.

And if *The Antiquary* looks back to the seventeenth century in
the shape of Ben Jonson, it recalls that age, particularly its earlier
decades, in its very heterogeneity. This is not to claim that what
we have in the novel is really a metaphysical poem in disguise, but
to maintain that the book's 'discordant juxtapositions', to quote
Robert C. Gordon again, are as much part of a worked-out
scheme (and demand of the reader a correspondingly flexible
attention) as parallel surprises in a fine poem of the earlier
seventeenth century. If one calls such conscious juxtapositions of
the incongruous 'mannerism', one can hardly describe it as '*careless* mannerism', but should rather see its calculated oddity as
'mannerist' in the sense in which that term is used of certain
poets, painters, and architects of the sixteenth and seventeenth
centuries.

The unifying principle behind the calculated oddity, I have
tried to suggest, is Scott's brooding over *vanitas vanitatum*.
Though the area within which the novel's action takes place is
extremely limited, it is Scott's Vanity Fair. I would argue, however, that its vision is at once kinder, fairer, and more mature than
Thackeray's. *All* is not vanity in *The Antiquary*. The society
which the novel depicts, in spite of its oddly assorted nature, does
fuse into a unity near the end, at the warning of invasion; compo-
nent parts do not just go their own selfish ways, though Scott prevents us from taking all this as a piece of solemn patriotic uplift
by making the alarm a false one. And there is Edie Ochiltree. I
have purposely avoided discussing him until now, as too many
accounts of *The Antiquary* give the impression that the novel
hardly exists apart from this character. Certainly he is a striking

creation, in whom stylized Scots vernacular is given a wide expressive range, from the pungently sardonic to the solemnly impressive. (Consider his admonition to Lovel and Hector M'Intyre before the duel, in Chapter 20.) But his true status cannot be appreciated unless he is very firmly placed in the context of the whole. For amidst so much that is vain, from the merely laughable to the wastefully tragic, he stands as a man embodying the absolute antithesis. Proud, indeed, he is; proud of his independence, proud of his ability to be useful to others – and pride of that kind is quite remote from vanity. He is no idealized figure; his life is anything but a pastoral idyll; he indulges in no Arcadian rhapsodizing about his lot. He has his perversities and foibles, to be sure, but of nothing that he says or does are we tempted to say 'What folly!' or 'What waste!' In Edie is symbolized the capacity to accept, to endure, and to be useful.

5

Scott and the Man of Prudence:
'Rob Roy'; 'Old Mortality'; 'The Abbot'

Probably few readers would immediately think of Edie Ochiltree as inhabiting the same kind of moral world as Mr Joshua Geddes in *Redgauntlet*. Though Edie is not perfect, he possesses none of those slightly suspect traits, makes us ask none of those rather awkward questions, which qualify our view of an apparently most admirable man. Yet there exists a relationship between them, a relationship pointing to one of Scott's central interests, though a relationship of something close to antithesis in the material scale. For in the very different ways that their respective circumstances permit, they are men of prudence.

Neither man can be seen as wholly governed by prudential considerations; neither is unable to take risks. There is nothing prudential, given the local situation, in Mr Geddes's erection of his fish-traps, or in Edie's coming to warn Sir Arthur and his daughter of their peril from the tide. But, whatever their human deviations from strict prudence, the two men can be said fundamentally to inhabit the same world of protective common sense, their sharing of which seems all the more vivid when one thinks of the huge disparity between them in material condition. Though both can be really roused on occasion, one has of them the feeling that they will survive when men of more rashly ardent temperament will rush headlong into disaster or at least only narrowly avoid it – usually through the aid of a prudential friend. Economically belonging to separate worlds, both are concerned in their different ways with the conditions of material survival. Independent and unselfish as he is, Edie Ochiltree knows too much about realities to forget that his ready usefulness is such a condition. And the firm religious tenets of Mr Geddes do not degenerate into a ranting, mindless enthusiasm that would alienate the world in which he is a successful man. Above all, both are men of peace, to say which is to imply nothing indolent or complacent.

The three novels I shall discuss briefly in this chapter illustrate in different ways Scott's preoccupation with what it is to be or to become a man of prudence. Brevity of treatment was suggested not because the books are negligible, though they are exceedingly uneven, but because their overall pattern of working has already been indicated, especially in the chapter on *Waverley*. In each of them a young man finds himself more or less involuntarily implicated in events of national significance, and is in one way or another divided in his sympathies. It will be seen, however, that the interest attaching to that centrally placed protagonist varies widely from novel to novel.

The idea of the prudential clearly exercised a highly non-Romantic fascination over Scott. It is not hard to see why this was. In some situations Scott was an astute man of business, and where the short term was concerned he could even be a prudent one. But he did fall into financial disaster after his years of greatest success, disaster which forced him into the assembly-line manufacture of books in order to pay his creditors; and however persuasively his biographical defenders may argue that such ruin was not in the strictest sense his fault, there can be no doubt that he did take, in a spirit of high adventure, very serious risks. It is one more of his complexities, yet a deeply understandable one, that such a man should so strikingly have been preoccupied in his fiction with the notion of prudence.

The more one thinks about *Rob Roy* the odder it seems. With the name of a famous Scottish outlaw for its title, and a deal of rugged landscape in its décor, the book has money at its very centre and at times positively smells of the counting-house. At its best the novel is quintessential Scott in its bringing together of incongruously disparate worlds. Its less satisfactory aspects may here be summarily disposed of – though one does not, unfortunately, sweep them out of the way quite so easily when actually reading it. They relate mainly to the two prominent female characters, Diana Vernon and Rob Roy's wife Helen MacGregor. The former was meant to be fascinating, and some appear actually to have found her so, but the reader interested in serious fiction will be more likely to judge her energetic verbiage to be a downright bore. As for Helen MacGregor, who was intended as a figure of frightening impressiveness, portentously mingling dignity with cruelty, Scott's melodramatic rendering has the effect of making her repulsively absurd.

Behind the action lie preparations for the unsuccessful Jacobite rising of 1715. *Rob Roy*, however, is fundamentally quite a different kind of book from *Waverley*. The Jacobite cause does not in itself bulk large as a central interest, but functions rather as a means of bringing together the Highland world of Rob Roy himself and the world of banking and commerce. From the strange, sometimes comically strange, juxtaposition of these worlds, the book derives its life.

To rehearse the plot would be superfluous. Let it suffice to say that it concerns the adventures of young Frank Osbaldistone, who does not want to follow in his enterprising father's financial footsteps, but who becomes involved with Rob Roy and his clansmen when his own treacherous cousin Rashleigh, taken into the firm in his stead, threatens it with commercial disgrace. Through the help of the outlaw, who is aware of Rashleigh's plans, disaster is averted.

Although Frank Osbaldistone is the narrator, he does not in himself have the same importance as Edward Waverley. He is akin to Waverley in that he travels from England to Scotland and finds himself involved in the kind of perilous adventure for which he has not bargained, but with that, significant resemblance stops. *Rob Roy* does not concern itself with Frank's education for maturity except in a marginal implicit way. Its essential organization rests on the use of three boldly representative characters. First there is the elder Osbaldistone, of the great London mercantile house of Osbaldistone and Tresham. Immensely successful and highly esteemed, he is yet no narrowly prudential moneymaker; indeed his life is characterized by the gusto with which he pursues his speculations:

Impetuous in his schemes, as well as skilful and daring, each new adventure, when successful, became at once the incentive, and furnished the means, for farther speculation. It seemed to be necessary to him, as to an ambitious conqueror, to push on from achievement to achievement, without stopping to secure, far less to enjoy, the acquisitions which he made. Accustomed to see his whole fortune trembling in the scales of chance, and dexterous at adopting expedients for casting the balance in his favour, his health and spirits and activity seemed ever to increase with the animating hazards on which he staked his wealth; and he resembled a sailor, accustomed to brave the billows and the foe, whose confidence rises on the eve of tempest and battle. (6)

If dexterity at adopting expedients be a kind of prudence, then Mr Osbaldistone, in a very special sense, is a man of prudence. So, within his utterly different context, in his mountain hideout remote from London and 'the dark counting-house in Crane Alley', is the outlaw Rob Roy. Certainly no man could be more adroit at extricating himself from situations of apparently desperate peril. Both men are nevertheless fundamental adventurers, with the further odd resemblance in overall dissimilarity that they are both men of 'honour'. To Rob Roy, as one would expect, 'honour' is pride, pride of name, of blood, of cause, the 'honour' won and defended by the sword. And whatever the obvious contextual differences, the Osbaldistone brand of 'honour' presents a close parallel. 'You do me injustice, Miss Vernon,' says Frank, when the girl chides him for showing acute distress at the news of Rashleigh's manoeuvre,

'I grieve not for the loss of the money, but for the effect which I know it will produce on the spirits and health of my father, to whom mercantile credit is as honour; and who, if declared insolvent, would sink into the grave, oppressed by a sense of grief, remorse, and despair, like that of a soldier convicted of cowardice, or a man of honour who had lost his rank and character in society.'
(163)

Between Crane Alley and the Highlands, between the merchant adventurer and the condemned outlaw, stands Bailie Nicol Jarvie of Glasgow, man of business and property (he has a farm in the West Indies, for instance), and self-styled man of prudence. Not for him the equating of mercantile credit with 'honour':

'But I maun hear naething about honour; we ken naething here but about credit. Honour is a homicide and a bloodspiller, that gangs about making frays in the street; but Credit is a decent honest man, that sits at hame and makes the pat play.'

ken know; *sits at hame and makes the pat play* sits at home and keeps the pot boiling

He is openly critical of the elder Osbaldistone's adventuring:

'Mr. Osbaldistone is a gude honest gentleman; but I aye said he was ane o' them wad make a spune or spoil a horn, as my father the worthy deacon used to say. The deacon used to say to me, "Nick – young Nick" (his name was Nicol as weel as mine; sae folk ca'd us in their daffin', young Nick and auld Nick) – "Nick," said he, "never put out your arm farther than ye can draw it easily back again." I hae said sae to Mr. Osbaldistone, and he didna seem to take it a'thegither sae kind as I wished – but it was weel meant – weel meant.'

(207)

gude good; *I aye said he was ane o' them wad make a spune or spoil a horn* I always said he was one of those who would either achieve great things or fail totally; *ca'd us in their daffin'* called us in their joking; *a'thegither* altogether; *weel* well

No wonder Frank remarks that 'This discourse, delivered with prodigious volubility, and a great appearance of self-complacency, as he recollected his own advice and predictions, gave little promise of assistance at the hands of Mr. Jarvie.'

The good bailie, however, is not prudential to the point of inhumanity. By the end of Chapter 26 Frank is able to report that he saw him 'gradually surmount the barriers of caution, under the united influence of public spirit and good-natured interest in our affairs', though his 'doughty resolution of taking the field in person, to aid in the recovery of my father's property' has behind it the prudential wish 'to avoid loss and acquire gain', for he stands to suffer if Mr Osbaldistone goes insolvent.

The resulting events show the bailie in postures of sometimes grotesque imprudence involving danger to life and limb (into which he has ironically been led partly by prudential considerations), or with bizarre good intentions proposing to Rob Roy such things as his helping the outlaw's sons into a 'respectable' position in trade, without any thought for the explosion of incredulous fury this must inevitably provoke! In some ways he understands Roy Roy, who is his kinsman, for the urban mercantile class he belongs to has not yet grown totally alien to the ties of ancient tradition, any more than his city of Glasgow can be unaware of the nearby Western Highlands. Yet the often comically prudential remains Mr Jarvie's abiding characteristic, as when he hesitates over the debt owed him by Rob Roy, feeling that he really ought not to insist on it, only to end by accepting the money according to his rooted principle that one must 'avoid loss and acquire gain'.

One of the last sights we have of Bailie Nicol Jarvie is when he and Frank are being rowed away from the Highlands down Loch Lomond. The young man, though sad at what then seems the final disappearance from his life of Diana Vernon, is impressed by the scenery. The bailie, we are told,

> had also his speculations, but they were of somewhat a different complexion, as I found when, after about an hour's silence, during which he had been mentally engaged in the calculations necessary, he undertook to prove the possibility of draining the lake, and 'giving to plough and harrow many hundred, ay, many a thousand acres, from whilk no man could get earthly gude e'enow, unless it were a gedd or a dish of perch now and then.'   (359)
>
> *whilk* which; *e'enow* just now

Here the principle of avoiding loss and acquiring gain leads the worthy Mr Jarvie to the extreme of prudential philistinism. And clearly Scott's handling of the prudential in the bailie's shape is nowhere very far from the satirical: satirical as in the passage just quoted, and also in those episodes which seem to demonstrate the near-impossibility of sustaining a consistently prudential policy, however apparently prudential one's driving motives. But although *Rob Roy* extracts a deal of comedy from the foibles of the prudential man, it would be a mistake to suppose that Scott means us to dismiss him. Jarvie may make us laugh, yet he is no fool; and his shortcomings are almost positive virtues by contrast with those of Frank Osbaldistone's ironically named servant, Andrew Fairservice, in whom the prudential descends to the level of the crudest expediency. Fairservice's impudently selfish behaviour performs the function of qualifying the satire at the bailie's expense. Let us not, says the author, laugh at the solidly prudential too loudly or too long. Many of us could well do with more of it than we have.

Old Mortality is commonly rated one of Scott's best novels by his modern enthusiasts. Certainly it should be read, for the book's treatment of politico-religious conflict in the late seventeenth century has great interest and much distinction. Between two extremes, Balfour of Burley on the puritan side, and Grahame of Claverhouse on the side of government, men bitterly opposed in principle yet akin, as Claverhouse admits, in ruthless fanaticism,

stands the moderate Henry Morton, from family tradition fundamentally sympathetic to the puritan cause, yet desperately wishing
for peace, law, and order. Scott uses this pattern of values with a
good deal of skill; the task of trying to present the claims of both
sides naturally appealed to the author of *Waverley*. But one may
feel that, whatever its virtues, *Old Mortality* is not quite as good a
novel as it ought to be. Re-reading can make its patterning come
to seem too neatly schematic, so that what was meant to serve the
purpose of being fair to both sides ends up by somewhat simplifying. The handling of the puritans, for instance, though Scott
plainly wanted to avoid dismissive scorn, often approaches too
near to caricature for comfort.

We see something of this weakness early in Chapter 16, when
the puritanically zealous old Mause Headrigg, standing with her
son Cuddie and Henry Morton on a hill beside a field of battle,
upbraids the preacher Gabriel Kettledrummle (whom she has
previously regarded as 'a Nazarite purer than snow') for not
hurling himself into the fray:

This expostulation implied a reproach on Mr. Kettledrummle, who, though
an absolute Boanerges, or son of thunder, in the pulpit, when the enemy were
afar, and indeed sufficiently contumacious, as we have seen, when in their
power, had been struck dumb by the firing, shouts, and shrieks, which now
arose from the valley, and – as many an honest man might have been, in a
situation where he could neither fight nor fly – was too much dismayed to
take so favourable an opportunity to preach the terrors of Presbytery, as the
courageous Mause had expected at his hand, or even to pray for the successful event of the battle. His presence of mind was not, however, entirely lost,
any more than his jealous respect for his reputation as a pure and powerful
preacher of the word.

'Hold your peace, woman!' he said, 'and do not perturb my inward medi-
tations and the wrestlings wherewith I wrestle. – But of a verity the shooting
of the foeman doth begin to increase! peradventure, some pellet may attain
unto us even here. Lo! I will ensconce me behind the cairn, as behind a strong
wall of defence.'   (181-2)

cairn a pile of stones erected as a memorial or a landmark

The preacher's convenient attributing of his inaction to 'the
wrestlings wherewith I wrestle' (which he knows will impress
Mause), and his use of sermon-like language when proposing
('Lo!') to protect himself from flying bullets, provoke the kind

of amusement which comes rather too easily to be relied on very often. No one need blame the poor man for preferring refuge to danger, after all, as Scott himself makes sufficiently plain in the first paragraph of the passage. Such prudence deserves no scorn. Cuddie Headrigg, however, though no zealot like his mother, thinks otherwise:

'He's but a coward body after a',' said Cuddie, who was himself by no means deficient in that sort of courage which consists in insensibility to danger; 'he's but a daidling coward body. He'll never fill Rumbleberry's bonnet. – Od! Rumbleberry fought and flyted like a fleeing dragon. It was a great pity, puir man, he couldna cheat the woodie. But they say he gaed singing and rejoicing till't, just as I wad gang to a bicker o' brose supposing me hungry, as I stand a gude chance to be. – Eh, sirs! yon's an awfu' sight, and yet ane canna keep their een aff frae it.' (182)

daidling dabbling, stupid; *flyted* raged, scolded; *gaed* went; *till't* to it; *bicker* bowl; *brose* Scottish dish somewhat resembling porridge; *ane canna keep their een aff frae it* one can't keep one's eyes away from it.

Cuddie's admirations are clear enough. If Kettledrummle falls short of Rumbleberry (and the name tells us what manner of person he was!) it is because he lacks the aggressive virtues. But Cuddie is more complex than a mere addiction to pugnacious energy in others would suggest. His 'insensibility to danger' may indicate a kind of stupidity, and certainly he is no great brain. He sees no incongruity in likening going to execution to satisfying one's hunger. Yet with the insensibility goes a tough realism, a realism exhibited by his comment on something that many would stop short of admitting – the fascination of carnage. And associated with this realism, despite his scorn for the prudential in Gabriel Kettledrummle, is a rooted philosophy which sees life's dangers as things to be avoided or escaped from by smart evasive action. What a pity, he remarks, that Rumbleberry 'couldna *cheat the woodie*', i.e. escape the gallows.

Much of what is most enduringly effective in *Old Mortality* centres on Cuddie Headrigg. Here he is with Henry Morton in Chapter 13, when that young man has just proclaimed his resistance to 'any authority on earth...that invades tyrannically my chartered rights as a freeman'. Cuddie wants to know what manner of 'charter' Morton invokes:

'The charter that I speak of,' said Morton, 'is common to the meanest

Scotchman. It is that freedom from stripes and bondage which was claimed, as you may read in Scripture, by the Apostle Paul himself, and which every man who is freeborn is called upon to defend, for his own sake and that of his countrymen.'

'Hegh, sirs!' replied Cuddie, 'it wad hae been lang or my Leddy Margaret, or my mither either, wad hae fund out sic a wiselike doctrine in the Bible! The tane was aye graning about giving tribute to Caesar, and the tither is as daft wi' her whiggery. I hae been clean spoilt, just wi' listening to twa blethering auld wives;'   (158)

mither mother; *fund* found; *the tane...the tither* the one...the other; *graning* groaning; *blethering* absurdly chattering; *auld* old

Cuddie's realism makes short work of those who 'interpret' Scripture to fit their own causes, whether it be Lady Margaret Bellenden, mistress of the barony on which he works, using the Bible in support of king and government, or old Mause his mother, finding therein proof positive that her own fanaticism is the true prophetic fire. But the irony extends to Morton as well, for might he not here be reprehended, if more mildly, for playing the same sort of game? Cuddie, however, has other matter to ventilate; he continues:

'but if I could get a gentleman that wad let me tak on to be his servant, I am confident I wad be a clean contrary creature; and I hope your honour will think on what I am saying, if ye were ance fairly delivered out o' this house of bondage, and just take me to be your ain wally-de-shamble' (valet de chambre).

Pathetically incongruous as this seems, for both are in captivity, Cuddie is being, so he thinks, prudentially opportunist. And as Morton's servant he subsequently insists on regarding himself, to the astonishment of his 'master' in Chapter 22, who receives into the bargain a lesson in making the most of war:

'Well, Cuddie, if you insist on taking the chance of my unprosperous fortunes' –

'Ou ay, I'se warrant us a' prosper weel eneugh,' answered Cuddie, cheeringly, 'an ance my auld mither was weel putten up. I hae begun the campaigning trade at an end that is easy eneugh to learn.'

'Pillaging, I suppose?' said Morton, 'for how else could you come by that portmanteau?'

'I wotna if it's pillaging, or how ye ca't,' said Cuddie; 'but it comes natural to a body, and it's a profitable trade.'   (227)

an ance my auld mither was weel putten up once my old mother was properly provided for

And when Morton wryly compliments him on having made 'a

very successful foray for a beginner', he exultantly replies 'Haena I e'en now?...I tauld ye I wasna that dooms (utterly) stupid, if it cam to lifting things.'

The 'insensibility', of course, is patent; the prudential may seem in Cuddie to have sunk even lower than in Andrew Fairservice. But while Cuddie comes nowhere near being held up as a model, the canny realism with which he operates, within his limits of sensibility and understanding, earns a certain respect. He knows how to survive, and without being *altogether* a rogue. In fact his function is very different from that of Andrew Fairservice, for if the latter prevents us, by contrast, from going too far in mockery of Bailie Nicol Jarvie, Cuddie sets a salutary limit on the admiration one may feel for the non-prudential idealism of Henry Morton, and also in a general way casts an ironic light on the heroics of both embattled sides in the book.

One would hardly wish to deny, nevertheless, that Cuddie's brand of the prudential is itself seen with a deal of comic irony. Making the best of civil war, using its situations to one's own advantage, may be pragmatically sensible. It is not, on the other hand, especially admirable. In *The Abbot* Scott's exploration of the prudential achieves a further dimension, so that what finally emerges seems to be less simple prudence than mature recognition of what is 'right' or 'sound'.

That said, the fact must be faced that as a whole *The Abbot* is a weaker book than either *Rob Roy* or *Old Mortality*. Many readers in the old days of Scott's unquestioned reputation would, indeed, have seen it as an infinitely weaker book, almost a failure but for its portrait of Mary Queen of Scots in her imprisonment at Lochleven Castle. The following piece of editorial commentary gives a representative view (the writer also has in mind this novel's predecessor *The Monastery*, about which one would certainly agree with him):

Their inferiority lay not so much in the choice of a subject, as in the continued exaggeration of trifles, the prominence of second-rate characters, the delay of the action by the multiplication of unnecessary details, and the prolongation of irrelevant colloquies. In some of these respects the 'Abbot' is less objectionable than the 'Monastery,' and the introduction of such a personage as Mary Queen of Scots gives hope that the novelist will again rise to the natural 'height of the grand argument' – of which he was so capable; but the occupation of the foreground so long by such a petulant child as Roland Graeme, and such a fanatic as his grandmother, who are both made use of apparently in despair, disappoints us – even the Abbot himself has but a second-rate *role* in the performance. (*The Abbot*, edited by the Rev. P. Hately Waddell, LL.D. (Edinburgh, n.d.))

The commentator's more general complaints are to a great extent justified, so also his stricture on the prominence of Magdalen Graeme, Roland's grandmother, who is ludicrously unbelievable – considerably more so than Helen MacGregor in *Rob Roy* – and a bore. About Roland Graeme himself, though, he must be accounted utterly wrong, so wrong indeed as to empty the book of such distinction as it possesses.

The Abbot belongs, generally speaking, to what I have termed the category of historical fantasia, and I would regard it, all in all, as one of the better specimens of the type. On the level of light reading the portrait of Mary is powerfully imagined, and vastly superior in interest to *Kenilworth*'s rendering of Queen Elizabeth. The religious conflicts in Reformation Scotland, with the monasteries despoiled and the Catholics barely managing to survive, come across vividly, to say which is to put one's finger on the element in the book which gives it a special place among the historical fantasias and almost lifts it out of the category. Religious discord in Scott's own time was no longer anywhere near the bitter and often bloody phenomenon we encounter in *The Abbot* or *Old Mortality*, but its acrimonious grumblings could still be heard and are by no means mute in the Scotland of today, let alone in other countries where considerably more than mere faint reverberations are involved. *The Abbot* is 'historical', therefore, in a sense which goes beyond the fact of its introducing Mary Queen of Scots.

In the midst of the discord moves Roland Graeme, reared a Catholic yet constantly exposed to the influence of the Reformed faith. Far more important to *The Abbot* than Frank Osbaldistone to *Rob Roy*, and at least as interesting as Henry Morton in *Old Mortality*, Roland undergoes an education which parallels, though it does not in detail resemble, that of Edward Waverley. The Rev. P. Hately Waddell was right to call him 'a petulant child'; where he erred was in not realizing the importance of this to Scott's design. What *The Abbot* shows is Roland changing from petulance to maturity, adjusting himself, at first from mainly prudential considerations but later from conviction, to the pressures of the age, and in so doing discovering his own true self.

Taken as a page by the Lady of Avenel, Roland the child is insufferably arrogant: 'It seemed, in truth, as if to command were his natural sphere, so easily did he use himself to exact and receive compliance with his humours.' (p. 20) Yet the same chapter tells us that he 'displayed that early flexibility both of body and mind which renders exercise, either mental or bodily, rather matter of sport than of study', a flexibility which suggests even at this stage a capacity to adjust and adapt. Moreover, if he can hardly be called prudent in his reply to Magdalen Graeme when she taxes him for wavering in his faith, he shows that he is beginning to think towards an independent view: 'I forget nothing of what I owe to you, my dearest mother; show me how my blood can testify my gratitude, and you shall judge if I spare it. *But blindfold obedience has in it as little merit as reason.*' (p. 80; my italics.)

Prudence and independence are very much at loggerheads in the early part of his subsequent career. When contemplating going to Edinburgh he tells himself that there 'I shall find the means of shaping my own course through this bustling world', but his reckless behaviour on arrival suggests anything but 'shaping'. Ironically it is through his being sent into the personal service of the imprisoned Mary that he learns what shaping his own course really means, under conditions which imply the apparent reverse of independence.

Little prudence, again, attaches to his ardent heroics after reaching Lochleven Castle, stupefied as he is by the fascination of his royal mistress: 'Roland Graeme, on whose youth, inexperience, and ardent sense of what was dignified and lovely the demeanour of so fair and high-born a lady wrought like the charm of a magician, stood rooted to the spot with surprise and interest, longing to hazard his life in a quarrel so fair as that which Mary Stewart's must needs be.' Yet only in the previous chapter (20) we find him reflecting on the dangerous implications of his position, sent by the regent into Mary's service and at the same time destined for it by a person utterly opposed to the regent, his grandmother Magdalen Graeme:

It was quite evident that he had, through various circumstances not under his control, formed contradictory connexions with both the contending factions by whose strife the kingdom was distracted, without being properly an adherent of either. . . . . It required very little reflection to foresee that these contradictory claims on his services might speedily place him in a situation where his honour as well as his life might be endangered.   (208)

Through facing the contradictions in his situation, Roland comes to deal with those of his own nature. After his initial romantically uncritical enthusiasm for Mary's cause, he begins to think for himself, though never does his loyalty to her as a person waver. Caught he is, indeed, between devotion to her on the one hand, and awakening doubts, on the other, regarding that faith which is hers and in which he has been bred. Going at first from the purely prudential motive of deceiving the Lady of Lochleven to the devotions led by the household's Protestant pastor, he gradually finds himself asking questions, questions such as this about the dispersal of the monks and the despoiling of their monasteries:

The mazes of polemical discussion again stretched themselves before the eye of his mind. Had these men justly suffered their exile as licentious drones, the robbers, at once, and disgrace of the busy hive; or had the hand of avarice and rapine expelled from the temple not the ribalds who polluted, but the faithful priests who served, the shrine in honour and fidelity?   (316)

And although he retains a deep personal respect for the abbot, Father Ambrosius, Roland is able to reflect, after a skilful piece of verbal legerdemain on the good man's part, 'that when the truth was spoken for the purpose of deceiving, it was little better than a lie in disguise'.

It would be unfair to accuse Roland of trimming. Abidingly loyal to both the queen and the abbot, he is among those defeated in the battle which sends Mary to England and her ultimate execution. Yet because he has never been a rigid fanatic he endures, to pursue a happy life, to take possession of his hereditary birthright, and to embrace at last that Reformed faith to which, we are told, 'the heart of Roland had secretly long inclined'. We need not see Scott as polemically taking sides. What counts in *The Abbot* is its celebration of that true flexibility which leads to mature judgement in whatever direction, as opposed to the destructive dogma of the fanatic.

6

The Poems

Scott's poetry is harder to recommend today than any other branch of his work. The temptation virtually to ignore it is strong. One may make out a seemingly convincing case for relatively weak novels, can make them sound in some way interesting, even though the actual reading of them will show up the case as an exercise in special pleading. The less desirable kind of Scott Revival criticism, indeed, fails in precisely that way. But with the poetry it is quite different. Whereas the not particularly scrupulous account of a poor novel may suggest that the book has a thematic interest, often of a sociological type, constituting a claim for it to be read, Scott's poetry contains very little that can be made to sound inviting. A reader who finds exciting stimulus in the counterpointing of varied notions of justice in *The Heart of Mid-lothian*, for example, will probably be the reader who in poetry values concentration, or density of verbal texture, or sharp clarity, or the capacity of a poem to bring into play a complexity of mutually differing but co-present emotions. In a word, such a reader will want a poem to *exercise* him. He will not necessarily be a reader who expects all good poetry to be 'like Donne and Hopkins', to take the familiar type of sneer at those who look for density. More likely will he be, when approaching Scott, to think in terms of a contemporary like Wordsworth or some earlier writer in whom the poet was well versed, such as Dryden. And Scott will probably disappoint him.

There is, of course, the other contemporary who was responsible for Scott's turning to the novel: Byron, whose popularity became a threat to Scott the poet. But the Byron we enjoy today is the magnificent satirist of *Don Juan* and *The Vision of Judgement*, rather than Scott's rival in Romantic narrative; and even by the standard of verse-tales like *The Corsair*, or *The Siege of Corinth*, Scott's *Marmion* or *The Lady of the Lake* will to many readers make a poor showing. Relatively cheap and dated though Byron's tales are, they have colour and energy, however luridly melodramatic, and a sheer force of personality, however vulgarly flamboyant, which Scott's are notably without. To be a sceptical Romantic was not an advantage to Scott when essaying the verse-tale; when it came to the writing of *Waverley* the exact opposite was the case.

I observed that Scott the narrative romancer will make a poor showing to 'many' readers when set beside Byron in the same role. The vagueness was deliberate. Perhaps a majority of those who read poetry at all are not attracted by the verse-tales of either writer, but those who are will probably be so on account of some markedly personal predilection: a penchant for poetic travelogue, maybe, in the case of Byron's, or an actual acquaintance with the geographical settings of Scott's. And although one may easily say that such things are not, or ought not to be, relevant to one's estimate of literature, one cannot so easily dismiss their influence over even the sophisticated reader. What has to be insisted upon is that a liking based upon some such predilection cannot be a reason for setting on a poem the kind of valuation which implies that all educated people should know it. Because I happen to live within a very short distance of that part of Scotland called the Trossachs, I find quite a deal to enjoy in *The Lady of the Lake*, for all the things in it which make me wince or inappropriately giggle; but it would never occur to me to recommend serious study of that poem, and not merely because most readers of the present book will in all likelihood never have set foot in west Perthshire. The simple truth is that *The Lady of the Lake* and the rest of the tales have, with one or two qualifications, too little to offer by way of permanent interest. With their battles, duels, and general heroics, they belong to the history of popular literary taste, and illuminate an age which found a thrill in the sight of a suit of armour or the contemplation of a ruined castle.

Wherein, then, lies the justification for this chapter, assuming that mere tidy 'completeness' would hardly warrant its inclusion? The answer is that among the quite considerable bulk of poems by Scott there are a few, a very few, pieces of rather special distinction. They are not, to be sure, enough to make him a great poet, but one would not wish to be without them. And since *The Lady of the Lake* has already been mentioned, the business of distinguishing and discriminating may well start there.

The staple of the poem's verse exhibits little of particular interest, little that invites the reader to pause and put his finger on this or that in the way of manifest verbal liveness. A fair sample of its evocative best is the Spenserian vision of sunrise over Stirling in the prelude to Canto Sixth:

> The sun, awakening, through the smoky air
> Of the dark city casts a sullen glance,
> Rousing each caitiff to his task of care,
> Of sinful man the sad inheritance;
> Summoning revellers from the lagging dance,
> Scaring the prowling robber to his den;
> Gilding on battled tower the warder's lance,
> And warning student pale to leave his pen,
> And yield his drowsy eyes to the kind nurse of men.

Or, to take something from the verse in which Scott conducts the main narrative, here is a characteristic example of efficiently picturesque décor:

> The western waves of ebbing day,
> Roll'd o'er the glen their level way;
> Each purple peak, each flinty spire,
> Was bathed in floods of living fire.
> But not a setting beam could glow
> Within the dark ravines below,
> Where twined the path in shadow hid,
> Round many a rocky pyramid,
> Shooting abruptly from the dell
> Its thunder-splinter'd pinnacle;   (Canto First)

Unfortunately such appealingly sensuous confections are outnumbered by the passages of heroic rant and bardic bluster, not to mention the lyrics which punctuate the story as regularly as songs in a 'musical'. Some of these are truly awful:

> 'Huntsman, rest! thy chase is done,
> While our slumbrous spells assail ye,
> Dream not, with the rising sun,
> Bugles here shall sound reveillé . . .'
>   (Canto First)

Yet one of the songs, proffered in the most unpromising context, brings *The Lady of the Lake* really to life. Singer and setting are pure popular Romanticism; we look in vain for the mixed attitudes surrounding Flora's recital to Waverley:

> Now wound the path its dizzy ledge
> Around a precipice's edge,
> When lo! a wasted female form,
> Blighted by wrath of sun and storm,
> In tatter'd weeds and wild array,
> Stood on a cliff beside the way,
> And glancing round her restless eye,
> Upon the wood, the rock, the sky,
> Seem'd nought to mark, yet all to spy.
> Her brow was wreath'd with gaudy broom;
> With gesture wild she waved a plume
> Of feathers, which the eagles fling
> To crag and cliff from dusky wing;   (Canto Fourth)

Meant to be wildly sublime, that passage ends by being grotesquely ludicrous. But the song is quite another matter:

> They bid me sleep, they bid me pray,
>   They say my brain is warp'd and wrung –
> I cannot sleep on Highland brae,
>   I cannot pray in Highland tongue.
> But were I now where Allan glides,
> Or heard my native Devan's tides,
> So sweetly would I rest and pray
> That heaven would close my wintry day!
>
> 'Twas thus my hair they bade me braid,
>   They made me to the church repair;
> It was my bridal morn they said,
>   And my true love would meet me there.
> But woe betide the cruel guile,
> That drown'd in blood the morning smile
> And woe betide the fairy dream!
> I only waked to sob and scream.

The singer is a Lowland maid (hence the references to the Lowland rivers Allan and Devan) taken captive on her wedding day, her bridegroom having been killed by the chief of the Highland raiders. What strikes one about the song is its simple starkness. It has the naked power of Wordsworth's best short poems about loss and violence, yet nothing in it is crudely lurid, as one might have expected it to be from the melodramatic context. The little poem, a real masterpiece in itself, owes its effect to the contrast between the monotonous metrical sing-song, the regularly ordered rhythmic frame of the verse, which builds up a rather lulling impression, and the suddenly revealed violence of the story. Associated with that is the further contrast between language redolent of the familiar tags of folk poetry ('And my true love would meet me there'), which, like the insistent beat of the metre, works somewhat against a sharp emotional focus, and the final harshly matter-of-fact record of personal anguish: 'I only waked to sob and scream.'

In his preface to *Lyrical Ballads* Wordsworth speaks of 'the tendency of metre to divest language, in a certain degree, of its reality, and thus to throw a sort of half consciousness of unsubstantial existence over the whole composition', and concludes that because of this 'there can be little doubt, but that more pathetic situations and sentiments, that is, those which have a greater proportion of pain connected with them, may be endured in metrical composition, especially in rhyme, than in prose'. The preface remains to this day a fine piece of exploratory analysis, but one must question the adequacy of what Wordsworth says in that passage. While the words 'a sort of half consciousness of unsubstantial existence' pretty fairly describe the *initial* effect produced by the rhythmic monotony in Blanche of Devan's song, it is totally wrong to suppose that the metre from which that monotony derives acts as a panacea, a sweetener of the pill, a softener of the agony. The metre in Scott's poem does not make the pain more endurable; it makes it, by the contrast I have sketched, all the more intense. Some of Wordsworth's own finest things ('She dwelt among the untrodden ways', 'Three years she grew in sun and shower') work in much the same way. The passage from the preface, then, though it raises a point of the first importance, offers only a half-convincing account of what metre does to the reader's response to a poem's subject-matter.

An even shorter lyric than Blanche of Devan's lament, Lucy Ashton's song from *The Bride of Lammermoor* (a novel I have not included in this study, since I consider it to have had more than its due of critical justice), has a similar distinction:

> Look not thou on beauty's charming, –
> Sit thou still when kings are arming, –
> Taste not when the wine-cup glistens, –
> Speak not when the people listens, –
> Stop thine ear against the singer, –
> From the red gold keep thy finger, –
> Vacant heart, and hand, and eye,
> Easy live and quiet die.

Throughout the first six lines Scott keeps up the same cadence, line after line, as injunction succeeds injunction. Then, when the procession of negatives has established a homilectic monotone, comes the change: 'Vacant heart, and hand, and eye'. Till that point every line has been a self-contained sentence, the insistent repetition of this pattern being the principal way in which the effect of homily is produced. But now the pattern breaks down. While one quickly sees that the line is part of a sentence which the final line completes (supplying the word 'with' before 'Vacant heart'), this does not invalidate the contrast resulting from its not being a sentence in itself like all its predecessors. Moreover each previous line has presented a single sweep of sense from beginning to end, without pause, without hesitation, so that although each is an injunction to abstain we have the impression that something is definitely being *said*. The singer is being negative in a very positive way, so to speak. Now, however, we have only the contemplation of vacancy. From a strictly metrical point of view the pattern remains basically intact, with four marked stresses to the line, but the rhythm is wholly altered. For one thing the line lacks the final syllable of its predecessors, and for another it breaks down their bold sweep into a swaying lilt. It is as though the sustained effort of making a series of definite pronouncements has proved too much for the singer, who now gladly lapses into the comforting sing-song of 'Easy live and quiet die.' Behind the poem, of course, is the pathetic situation of the girl in the novel from which it comes, yet the poignancy of this plea for the extinction of all desire and ambition comes across independently – a poignancy made all the sharper by our sense of its being only barely contained within the incantatory verse whose cadences recall the 'Dies irae':

> Day of wrath and day of mourning,
> See fulfilled the prophet's warning

Lucy Ashton's song has long been admired, though one would not immediately associate it with the criticism of the last thirty years, in Cambridge or anywhere else. With another song from a novel, this time *The Heart of Midlothian*, the case is different. In *Education and the University* (Chatto and Windus, London, 1943) we find F. R. Leavis pointing to 'the type-contrast between Scott's *Proud Maisie* and Cory's *Heraclitus*...the contrast between the poem that seems to state and present barely without emotional comment, the emotion being generated between the parts when the reader has them in his mind, and the poem that is overtly emotional and incites directly to a "moved" response, the emotion seeming to lie out there on the page.' (p. 83) Here, then, is Scott's poem:

> Proud Maisie is in the wood,
>   Walking so early;
> Sweet Robin sits on the bush,
>   Singing so rarely.
>
> 'Tell me, thou bonny bird,
>   When shall I marry me?' –
> 'When six braw gentlemen
>   Kirkward shall carry ye.'
>
> 'Who makes the bridal bed,
>   Birdie, say truly?' –
> 'The grey-headed sexton
>   That delves the grave duly.
>
> 'The glow-worm o'er grave and stone
>   Shall light thee steady,
> The owl from the steeple sing,
>   "Welcome, proud lady."'

As Leavis says, the poem seems simply to state what happened in the imagined encounter between Maisie and the redbreast, baldly to record their dialogue. Nothing overtly tells us what the poem's emotional significance may be; it is left to the reader to infer what the situation must mean for the 'proud lady'.

Anything like an attempt at full analysis of such a piece runs the risk of insulting the reader's intelligence, so consummately successful is Scott in presenting just enough information for the poem's tissue of significance to be deduced. But a few pointers to the kind of speculation towards which Scott directs us may be suggested. One starts with the poem's central irony: that Maisie's bridal bed will be her grave and her bridegroom death. The reader naturally tends to assume that Maisie understands what the bird means, and certainly one way of reading the poem is to imagine her horror at that mocking welcome of the last line, horror at the realization that her pride is to be brought low by her extinction as a live human being. As soon as we have said that, of course, the poem strikes us as having a further facet, that of a moral fable of the 'Pride before a Fall' variety. Yet nothing in the poem openly tells us that it is designed to preach a lesson.

To go back to Maisie's response to the redbreast's prophecy, there is no absolute guarantee, despite the strong probability, that she understands it as we do. The meaning for her of the bird's last six lines may certainly seem too clear to be missed, but let us remember the essential fact of her *pride*, a fact insisted upon in the opening and closing lines which frame the whole poem. May she not, one ponders, be perhaps so utterly blinded by pride as not to realize what the bird is getting at? Unlikely, no doubt, but not impossible. A proud person wholly taken up with herself and her own future could not inconceivably be blinkered against grasping the prophecy that she will never be a bride in any ordinary sense. And to say that Maisie will never, in a normal way, a non-metaphorical way, be married, is to widen the poem's scope again. What might be termed the 'shock value' of its conclusion tempts us to suppose that Maisie's marriage to death is not far off. Yet one can find no absolute justification for this. Indeed the poem becomes in a way considerably more poignant if one fixes her death at the end of three-score-years-and-ten, after a lifetime of unwedded loneliness, a loneliness one might imagine her to be dreading. Why, after all, is she 'Walking so early'?

With those suggestions detailed discussion of *Proud Maisie* had better stop. Enough should have been said, however, to indicate just how concentrated a work that poem is. But it ought not to be left without some attention to its relationship with the traditional ballads which Scott knew so well. Clearly its method of working, its way of yielding significance bit by bit, its manner of implying a moral import rather than stating it overtly, bring it very close to such a genuine ballad as *The Demon Lover* (see my discussion of that poem in Chapter 3 of *Understanding Literature* (Cambridge, 1965)). As it happens, Scott included a ballad with interesting resemblances to *Proud Maisie* in his own *Minstrelsy of the Scottish Border*, his first important publication and a thoroughly enjoyable book, both for the poems themselves and the collector's information about them, whatever the scholarly shortcomings. Here is *Proud Lady Margaret* as Scott prints it, with his introductory remarks:

This ballad was communicated to the Editor by Mr. Hamilton, music-seller, Edinburgh, with whose mother it had been a favourite. Two verses and one line were wanting, which are here supplied from a different ballad having a plot somewhat similar. These verses are the 6th and 9th.

'Twas on a night, an evening bright,
　　When the dew began to fa',
Lady Margaret was walking up and down,
　　Looking o'er her castle wa'.

She looked east, and she looked west,
　　To see what she could spy,
When a gallant knight came in her sight,
　　And to the gate drew nigh.

'You seem to be no gentleman,
　　You wear your boots so wide;
But you seem to be some cunning hunter,
　　You wear your horn so syde.'

'I am no cunning hunter,' he said,
　　'Nor ne'er intend to be;
But I am come to this castle
　　To seek the love of thee;
And if you do not grant me love,
　　This night for thee I'll die.'

'If you should die for me, sir knight,
    There's few for you will mane,
For mony a better has died for me,
    Whose graves are growing green.

'But ye maun read my riddle,' she said,
    'And answer my questions three;
And but ye read them right,' she said,
    'Gae stretch ye out and die. –

'Now what is the flower, the ae first flower,
    Springs either on moor or dale?
And what is the bird, the bonnie bonnie bird,
    Sings on the evening gale?'

'The primrose is the ae first flower,
    Springs either on moor or dale;
And the thistlecock is the bonniest bird,
    Sings on the evening gale.'

'But what's the little coin,' she said,
    'Wald buy my castle bound?
And what's the little boat,' she said,
    'Can sail the world all round?'

'O hey, how many small pennies
    Make thrice three thousand pound?
Or hey, how mony small fishes
    Swim a' the salt sea round.'

'I think ye maun be my match,' she said,
    'My match, and something mair;
You are the first e'er got the grant
    Of love frae my father's heir.

'My father was lord of nine castles,
    My mother lady of three;
My father was lord of nine castles,
    And there's nane to heir but me.

'And round about a' thae castles,
    Ye may baith plow and saw,
And on the fifteenth day of May
    The meadows they will maw.'

'O hald your tongue, Lady Margaret,' he said,
   'For loud I hear you lie!
Your father was lord of nine castles,
   Your mother was lady of three;
Your father was lord of nine castles,
   But ye fa' heir to but three.

'And round about a' thae castles,
   You may baith plow and saw,
But on the fifteenth day of May
   The meadows will not maw.

'I am your brother Willie,' he said,
   'I trow ye ken na me;
I came to humble your haughty heart,
   Has gar'd sae mony die.'

'If ye be my brother Willie,' she said,
   'As I trow weel ye be,
This night I'll neither eat nor drink,
   But gae alang wi' thee.'

'O hold your tongue, Lady Margaret,' he said,
   'Again I hear you lie;
For ye've unwashen hands, and ye've unwashen feet,
   To gae to clay wi' me.

'For the wee worms are my bedfellows,
   And cauld clay is my sheets;
And when the stormy winds do blow,
   My body lies and sleeps.'

syde long or low; *unwashen hands...unwashen feet* alluding to the custom of washing and dressing dead bodies

Quite apart from that ballad's interest in connection with *Proud Maisie*, Scott's insertion of two stanzas from another source provides an additional excuse for giving it here in full, since his editorial treatment makes it, in a sense, partly his own poem. To put it more exactly, his procedure is that of the genuine folk-singer of oral tradition, who, when affected by loss of memory, either improvises his own verses to fill the gap or incorporates what seems appropriate material from another ballad. And to say that is to stress the closeness to traditional modes which makes the Scott of *Proud Maisie* so much more than an accomplished faker of 'the real thing'. At the same time, *Proud Maisie* clearly is a finer 'thing' than *Proud Lady Margaret*, a more compactly satisfying construct. Comparison in detail would be unfair, since the latter does depend for so much of its effect upon a lengthy drawing out, with the supernatural revelation, as in so many ballads, coming at the end. Nevertheless one can point to features of the poem – the initial setting of scenes followed by dialogue, the inch-by-inch emergence of the truth, the moral significance – that Scott has taken over and used with extraordinarily powerful economy in *Proud Maisie*, to produce an intensity of concentration absent from the necessarily far more expansive *Proud Lady Margaret*. And I think that where the question of moral significance is concerned one may quite fairly make a straight comparison to the credit of *Proud Maisie*, which achieves its comment on pride without the explicitness of Willie's 'I came to humble your haughty heart.' *Proud Maisie*, indeed, stands as that remarkable phenomenon, a poem which somehow *is* a real ballad while being quite plainly a work of sophisticated art.

Scott must have intended the songs in his novels to perform a function similar to that of the lyrics in Shakespeare's plays. With the best of them a sense of appropriate commentary does come across. The switch from delusion to stern reality which we find in *Proud Maisie* has close relevance to many a situation in *The Heart of Midlothian*. Likewise with another successful though less concentrated ballad-like poem from *Waverley*:

> Young men will love thee more fair and more fast;
> *Heard ye so merry the little bird sing?*
> Old men's love the longest will last,
> *And the throstle-cock's head is under his wing.*
>
> The young man's wrath is like light straw on fire;
> *Heard ye so merry the little bird sing?*
> But like red-hot steel is the old man's ire,
> *And the throstle-cock's head is under his wing.*
>
> The young man will brawl at the evening board;
> *Heard ye so merry the little bird sing?*
> But the old man will draw at the dawning the sword,
> *And the throstle-cock's head is under his wing.*

To find examples of situations illustrating what Davie Gellatley, the singer, has to say about young men, presents no difficulty to the reader of *Waverley*. Nor is it hard to see the bearing upon them of the second-line refrain: the chirping of little birds relates easily enough to youthful emotional ephemera. More subtle is the second refrain's function, though a few moment's thought conjures up the Baron of Bradwardine among the references to old men, with the idea of slumbering energy, formidable when roused, figured in the, at first seemingly irrelevant, words about the sleeping throstle-cock. (The baron's enduring 'love', of course, is for the feudal past embodied in the Jacobite cause, as opposed to Waverley's swiftly awakened but short-lived enthusiasm.) The song has a pointed effectiveness, but unlike *Proud Maisie* it is not especially memorable outside the novel. The reader might look out for the sprinkling of similarly functional poems when exploring the fiction.

Actually to call Davie Gellatley's song ballad-like is incorrect. Though the use of refrain gives it a folkish quality, the poem differs from a ballad in not telling a story, and in having that artfully sophisticated relationship between statement and refrain just discussed. If the concentrated assimilation of ballad technique in *Proud Maisie* may in a sense be termed sophisticated, it is not a sophistication lying anywhere near the surface. Scott knew very well the difference between the genuine traditional poem and that which seeks to pass itself off as such. In the 'Essay on Imitations of the Ancient Ballad' introducing Volume 3 of *Minstrelsy of the Scottish Border*, he has this to say about Shakespeare's 'Come away, come away, death':

In *Twelfth Night* he (Shakespeare) describes a popular ballad with a beauty and precision which no one but himself could have affixed to its character; and the whole constitutes the strongest appeal in favour of that species of poetry which is written to suit the taste of the public in general, and is most naturally preserved by oral tradition. But the remarkable part of the circumstance is, that when the song is actually sung by Feste the clown it differs in almost all particulars from what we might have been justified in considering as attributes of a popular ballad of that early period. It is simple, doubtless, both in structure and phraseology, but is rather a love song – a love song, also, which, though its imaginative figures of speech are of a very simple and intelligible character, may nevertheless be compared to anything rather than the boldness of the preceding age, and resembles nothing less than the ordinary minstrel ballad.

(*Minstrelsy of the Scottish Border* (Harrap, London, 1931))

Davie Gellatley's poem is no love song, but what Scott says about the 'imaginative figures of speech', however simple, in 'Come away, come away, death', is relevant to the former.

To return to *Waverley*, Flora's Gaelic verses are little more than picturesque bluster:

> There is mist on the mountain, and night on the vale.
> But more dark is the sleep of the sons of the Gael.
> A stranger commanded – it sunk on the land,
> It has frozen each heart, and benumb'd every hand!

In another part of the novel, however, we find these very different stanzas 'To an oak tree, in the churchyard of – , in the highlands of Scotland, said to mark the grave of Captain Wogan, killed in 1649':

> Emblem of England's ancient faith,
> Full proudly may thy branches wave,
> Where loyalty lies low in death,
> And valour fills a timeless grave.

> And thou, brave tenant of the tomb!
> Repine not if our clime deny,
> Above thine honour'd sod to bloom,
> The flowerets of a milder sky.

> These owe their birth to genial May;
> Beneath a fiercer sun they pine,
> Before the winter storm decay –
> And can their worth be type of thine?

One need not quote the whole to give the characteristic quality. This may not be major poetry, yet what at first sight perhaps looks like rather perfunctory formal rhetoric has behind it a crisp precision, an urbane balance, which give the stanzas a surprisingly enduring strength. Though their reference is to a soldier who lived in the seventeenth century, their quality is wholly that of the eighteenth century in which Scott was born. The conclusion of Samuel Johnson's verses 'On the Death of Mr. Robert Levett' should clinch the point:

> His virtues walk'd their narrow round,
> Nor made a pause, nor left a void;
> And sure the Eternal Master found
> The single talent well employ'd.
>
> The busy day – the peaceful night,
> Unfelt, unclouded, glided by;
> His frame was firm – his powers were bright,
> Though now his eightieth year was nigh.
>
> Then with no fiery throbbing pain,
> No cold gradations of decay,
> Death broke at once the vital chain,
> And freed his soul the nearest way.

Johnson's verses *are* major poetry; Scott's are without that flexibility, that quality of 'wit', which permits the Biblical pun on 'talent' in an entirely serious tribute. But they exhibit what is basically the same kind of urbanely pointed and cultivated ease.

In the introductory epistles to the six cantos of *Marmion* a similar note is struck. *Marmion* itself, like *The Lady of the Lake*, will doubtless always be read by those who have their extra-literary reasons for enjoying it, and it would be snobbery to argue against that. The epistles, though, despite their incidental references to the main narrative, deserve attention as poems in their own right. Cosily intimate, moving easily from boyhood reminiscence to politics, from sharply etched landscape sketches to history, from the private world to the public, they are happy examples of the art of talking in verse. There is no need to exaggerate their claims to bring home the felicity of such things as this address to a bookish friend:

> How just that, at this time of glee,
> My thoughts should, Heber, turn to thee!
> For many a merry hour we've known,
> And heard the chimes of midnight's tone.
> Cease, then, my friend! a moment cease,
> And leave these classic tomes in peace!
> Of Roman and of Grecian lore,
> Sure mortal brain can hold no more.
> These ancients, as Noll Bluff might say,

'Were pretty fellows in their day;'
But time and tide o'er all prevail –
On Christmas eve a Christmas tale –

And when the mood is more sombre, the verse's cultivated crispness precludes any suggestion of mawkishness:

When, musing on companions gone,
We doubly feel ourselves alone,
Something, my friend, we yet may gain;
There is a pleasure in this pain:
It soothes the love of lonely rest,
Deep in each gentler heart impress'd.
'Tis silent amid worldly toils,
And stifled soon by mental broils;
But, in a bosom thus prepared,
Its still small voice is often heard,
Whispering a mingled sentiment,
'Twixt resignation and content.

(Introduction to Canto Second)

Sparse though the worthwhile achievements of Scott the poet may be, then, they are far from negligible. Nor, one realizes, are they so remote from the best of contemporaries and admired predecessors as one might have thought.

7

A note on Scott as critic: postscript

In Mr Ioan Williams's useful introduction to the pieces he has collected under the title *Sir Walter Scott on Novelists and Fiction*, we find what may initially strike us as a surprising reflection: 'Scott saw the English novel not as an isolated and purely national phenomenon, but as part of a continuous European tradition of prose fiction...He respected the unique position of Bunyan in the history of English fiction, but he was aware, as the modern reader is not normally aware, of the fact that *The Pilgrim's Progress* and *La Princesse de Clèves* were published in the same year.' After so much emphasis on the local and traditional, one realizes that Scott was, after all, decidedly a *European*. It is yet another aspect of his complexity.

All students of Scott will be grateful for this most valuable volume, which gathers together the essays contributed to *Ballantyne's Novelists Library* (with most of the purely biographical matter excised, but covered in the notes where necessary), a collection of reviews of works published during the author's lifetime, and passages from the prefatory material written for his own novels.

It would be a mistake to rate Scott's criticism, even at its best, too high. As Mr Williams points out, there are crudities and superficialities of outlook in some respects, which make certain kinds of literary effect seemingly inaccessible to him. He often disconcerts one by the juxtaposition of real penetration with matter that is at best merely decent and at worst platitudinous. Mr Williams remarks that Scott's view of the relationship between the novel and morality was a limited one, and an element of crudeness colours all his discussions of the subject. Yet he can be capable of this, in the piece on Samuel Richardson: 'But we have elsewhere intimated an opinion, that the direct and obvious moral to be deduced from a fictitious narrative, is of much less consequence to the public, than the mode in which the story is treated in the course of details.'

Some crudeness is apparent even there, of course, as it is, more distressingly, in the Fielding essay Scott refers to at the beginning of the sentence. But take away the words 'to the public', which imply an unnecessarily sweeping cynicism about the way in which novels are received and consequently about the way in which they are designed (Scott is often shamefaced over claiming for novels much more than 'entertainment value'), and we have a suggestive indication of the ability of works of literature to convey an implicit moral significance, rather than a 'direct and obvious' one, through their organization, their marshalling of minute particulars.

A good deal of what Scott has to offer goes little beyond the simplest kind of plot-summary, yet again and again one is struck, in the midst of this, by the rightness of his judgement and the felicity with which it finds expression. He admirably characterizes the special originality of Richardson: 'a cautious, deep, and minute examinator of the human heart...[who] like Cooke or Parry, left neither head, bay, nor inlet behind him, until he had traced its soundings, and laid it down in his chart, with all its minute sinuosities, its depths, and its shallows.' The imagery there, it should be noted, is not pure decoration but serves a critically descriptive purpose. Again, his analysis of Defoe's realism has a soundness and clarity of vision as to the means employed to produce verisimilitude that anticipates the classic essay by Leslie Stephen in *Hours in a Library*:[1] 'if...[a] fact be told by a man of plain sense, and sufficient knowledge of the world, the minuteness with which he tells the story, mixing up with it a number of circumstances, which are not otherwise connected with it, than as existing at the same moment, seems to guarantee the truth of what he says.' Writing on Sterne he pays due tribute to the individuality of 'one of the most affected, and one of the most simple writers...one of the greatest plagiarists, and one of the most original geniuses, whom England has produced', yet also censures that strain of nastiness in Sterne in a manner not

[1] Leslie Stephen, *Hours in a Library*, Vol. 1 (London, 1874).

easy to refute: 'A handful of mud is neither a firebrand nor a stone; but to fling it about in sport, argues coarseness of mind, and want of common manners.' The Jane Austen essay, on the other hand, is on the whole disappointing. All credit should go to Scott for recognizing so rarely distinguished a genius, but his critical limitations are badly in evidence when he takes her to task for dwelling too long on the 'prosing' of Mr Woodhouse and Miss Bates in *Emma*, assuming Jane Austen to be merely concerned with 'minute detail' and failing to see that the tiresomeness of those characters plays a deliberately planned part in the judgements that the book's organization makes us arrive at with regard to the heroine's behaviour.

The essays on such writers as Mrs Radcliffe, Horace Walpole, and Maturin, have more of a 'period' interest than anything else. They have their place in the history of criticism and the history of taste, without, however, throwing much light on Scott's use of material redolent of the Tales of Terror in his own work. Nor, it must be said, does one find any real help over this in his justification of a particularly irritating apparition, the White Lady of Avenel in *The Monastery*, though the piece is a fascinating example of sophisticated special pleading. Scott seems to have felt a certain guilt about the 'Gothic' element in his work, and never succeeded in justifying it, even to himself.

Scott reviewing himself, however, in the essay on *Tales of my Landlord*, is invaluable, and nowhere more so than when a deliberate instance of 'misunderstanding' or narrowly adverse criticism is employed to highlight important aspects of his own art. To the public of 1817, 'the author of *Waverley*', despite the suspicions of some, was a figure of mystery, so that Scott was able to write publicly about his work with all the appearance of bland disinterestedness, while in fact subtly indicating ways in which it should correctly be read. Thus the reviewer's comments on 'the insipidity of this author's heroes', though offered on the surface as an outsider's limiting criticism, are really part of an essential analysis of the functional use of such characters as Edward Waverley – essential, that is, to anyone believing, as Scott's self-reviewing gives ample warrant, that he genuinely could be a conscious artist, for all the assumption of 'carelessness' often underlying the overt statements of this so richly contradictory man.

I have chosen to reproduce my own review of Mr Williams's book with only very small alterations, partly because the volume is the most useful and accessible collection of Scott's criticism now available, and also because I think it says what needs to be said about Scott's critical strength and weakness without the possibly blunting effect of revision designed to conceal the article's original purpose. And the strength and the weakness are largely those of the non-critical work. We admire Scott's flexible intelligence, his tolerant understanding, his sense of life's complexities; yet, as I remarked in connection with *Old Mortality*, we can often feel that the work is somehow not quite as good as it ought to be. Scott ought *not* to have allowed *The Heart of Midlothian* to fall off as it does; he *ought* to have seen what Jane Austen was doing with Miss Bates and Mr Woodhouse. But the works are as they are, and one has to accept them as such.

It is hoped that this short study has said enough about their virtues to make new readers want to accept some of them, in spite of the reservations which acceptance must involve. No doubt it could be urged that my selection of works, *Waverley* and *The Heart of Midlothian* apart, displays a measure of perversity. Does not *Redgauntlet* deserve a chapter to itself? Can I justify including *The Abbot* while leaving out *The Bride of Lammermoor*? – Those are likely queries. My answer can only be that although I have tried to put most emphasis upon what is incontrovertibly distinguished in Scott, my endeavour to isolate for inspection particular interests that seem likely to recommend him to the serious modern reader has inevitably led me to novels such as *Guy Mannering* and *The Abbot*, in which those interests are peculiarly evident, though surrounded by relatively inferior material. Maybe *Redgauntlet* could have been studied at greater length, but the book's significance and mode of working did not strike me as requiring the fairly full analysis accorded to *Waverley*. *The Bride of Lammermoor*, marred by overdone 'atmosphere', should be read in connection with Scott's interest in social change (it has links with *Guy Man-*

nering), and *A Legend of Montrose*, though burdened with a deal of exasperating melodrama, contains in the person of Dugald Dalgetty a superbly comic embodiment of prudential expediency (see *The Author of Waverley*, by D. D. Devlin (Macmillan, London, 1971)).

For the rest, *The Fortunes of Nigel* oscillates between the good and bad, but is among the very best of the historical fantasias and contains some passages of great expressive originality. Like *The Abbot* it sometimes threatens to leap out of its category. And *Woodstock*, if tiresome for quite long stretches, deserves attention at a far more serious level than the once widely current *Kenilworth* or *The Talisman*.

But my final emphasis must be on something whose worth requires no qualification. 'Wandering Willie's Tale' from *Redgauntlet* has a classic perfection of its own; relevant though it is to the novel from which it comes, the tale is a detachable entity. If *Proud Maisie* is Scott's own traditional ballad, we can use the same paradox and point to this as his own folk-tale. One cannot easily write 'about' it, for Scott's marvellous achievement lies in the way he has caught the varying tones of the narrator's imagined voice, from the cannily sarcastic to the gravely solemn. All one can really say is 'Read it, and try to *hear* it as you read.' Because the tale has such unity – the unity given by the narrative voice – illustrative quotation is no easier than comment. The following extract, telling of Steenie Steenson's encounter with a stranger, a stranger of whose identity we are in little doubt, may however convey something of the story's extraordinarily easy capacity to move from the humdrum to the abnormal, from the real to the fantastic:

On he rode, little caring where. It was a dark night turned, and the trees made it yet darker, and he let the beast take its ain road through the wood; when, all of a sudden, from tired and wearied that it was before, the nag began to spring, and flee, and stend, that my gudesire could hardly keep the saddle; upon the whilk, a horseman, suddenly riding up beside him, said, 'That's a mettle beast of yours, freend; will you sell him?' So saying, he touched the horse's neck with his riding-wand, and it fell into its auld heighho of a stumbling trot. 'But his spunk's soon out of him, I think,' continued the stranger, 'and that is like mony a man's courage, that thinks he wad do great things till he come to the proof.'

My gudesire scarce listened to this, but spurred his horse, with 'Gude e'en to you, freend.'

But it's like the stranger was ane that doesna lightly yield his point; for, ride as Steenie liked, he was aye beside him at the selfsame pace. At last my gudesire, Steenie Steenson, grew half angry, and, to say the truth, half feared. 'What is it that ye want with me, freend?' he said. 'If you be a robber, I have nae money; if ye be a leal man, wanting company, I have nae heart to mirth or speaking; and if ye want to ken the road, I scarce ken it mysell.'

'If you will tell me your grief,' said the stranger, 'I am one that, though I have been sair misca'd in the world, am the only hand for helping my freends.'

So my gudesire, to ease his ain heart, mair than from any hope of help, told him the story from beginning to end.

'It's a hard pinch,' said the stranger; 'but I think I can help you.'

'If you could lend me the money, sir, and take a lang day – I ken nae other help on earth,' said my gudesire.

'But there may be some under the earth,' said the stranger. 'Come, I'll be frank wi' you; I could lend you the money on bond, but you would maybe scruple my terms. Now, I can tell you that your auld laird is disturbed in his grave by your curses, and the wailing of your family, and if ye daur venture to go to see him, he will give you the receipt.'

My gudesire's hair stood on end at this proposal, but he thought his companion might be some humoursome chield that was trying to frighten him, and might end with lending him the money. Besides, he was bauld wi' brandy, and desperate wi' distress; and said he had courage to go to the gate of hell, and a step farther, for that receipt.

The stranger laughed.

stend leap, take long steps; *gudesire* grandfather; *mettle* fine, spirited; *freend* friend; *leal* decent, with good intentions; *misca'd* given a bad name; *daur* dare; *bauld* bold

And to hell, in effect, Steenie goes, to come to his senses eventually 'in the auld kirkyard of Redgauntlet parochine (parish), just at the door of the family aisle'. Had Scott written nothing else, 'Wandering Willie's Tale' would have ensured him a unique place in literature.